Infinite Difference

Infinite Difference

Other Poetries by UK Women Poets

edited by

Carrie Etter

Shearsman Books
Exeter

First published in the United Kingdom in 2010 by
Shearsman Books Ltd
58 Velwell Road,
Exeter EX4 4LD

ISBN 978-1-84861-099-6
First Edition

CONTENTS

for my nieces—

Katelyn, Kaylee, Lindsey, Sara and Josslyn—

in all their possibility

Introduction

This anthology gathers poetries not readily found in the pages of Britain's broadsheets or larger-circulation literary journals. More implicitly, *Infinite Difference* makes the case that Britain's tendency to divide poetry into the categories of "Mainstream" and "Experimental" or "Avant Garde" undermines our sense of the rich array of poetries being written. While this range might place at one end a linear narrative poem, and at the other end a fragmented, associative one, the land between is rich and various. The expanse might be further evidenced by suggesting different extremes as points of reference, such as the degree of engagement with the natural environment. The poetries being written in Britain today might in fact be regarded as being on a spectrum holding infinite points of difference, and this anthology as bringing to a larger audience work on that spectrum that has had limited, if not quite ultraviolet, visibility.[1]

While it is beyond the scope of this introduction to survey the reception of this division as it operates in the United States and the UK, one indicator is telling. A significant difference between the poetry culture of the United States and that of the United Kingdom is that work regarded as Other to the Mainstream, in the UK, never receives established prizes.[2] The most recognized awards for poetry in the UK are the T. S. Eliot Prize, the Costa Prize, and the Forward Prize, for individual books. Even those Other poets who have gained international acclaim have never made the shortlists for these prizes, and now, certain it will merely waste time and money, some publishers forego sending their non-Mainstream work for prize consideration at all.[3]

With these prizes and their shortlistings come review articles in national newspapers such as *The Times, The Guardian*, and *The Independent*, invitations for readings at festivals and universities, and commissions, among other forms of critical and financial support. A poet whose work is regarded as of the Mainstream has a far greater chance of obtaining these opportunities than one whose poetry is not. This is to say that in Britain, poetry's cultural capital remains squarely with the Mainstream, or the most commonly written poetries.

While this account begins to explain why the work herein has not received much notice in this country, a further question remains: Why focus on women? Isn't a women's anthology unnecessary, particularly in British poetry where one can easily name prominent women writers such as Moniza Alvi, Carol Ann Duffy, Selima Hill, Sinéad Morrissey, Alice Oswald and many more?

In her introduction to *Women's Work: Modern Women Poets Writing in English,* Eva Salzman argues convincingly for the continued need for women's anthologies, by reviewing the surprisingly low proportions of women to men in even the most recent anthologies and by recounting the still dismissive and gendered critical language often used to describe women's poetry.[4] In the second part of her essay, focusing on the work in the anthology and the scope of modern poetry by women, Salzman notes that many of them have been inspired by the Black Mountain Poets, the New York Poets, and Language poets. While a few such poets are acknowledged and included, such as Lyn Hejinian, Fanny Howe, and Lorine Niedecker, Salzman's choice of comparatively normative poems by these women obscures the extent of their variety and range. *Women's Work* provides an array of poetries and numerous fine poems, but its scope is limited to the more Mainstream end of the spectrum, with unrepresentative poems from poets who tend to work outside it; it also extends beyond Britain to include other Anglophone poets, especially American.

Looking specifically at the position of Other women poets in the UK, in its October 2007 edition *Jacket* published the forum "Post-Marginal Positions: Women and the UK Experimental/Avant-Garde Poetry Community," moderated by Catherine Wagner.[5] Here such poets as Andrea Brady and Geraldine Monk offered possible explanations for the relative absence of women outside the Mainstream in the UK, as compared to the States. As Emily Critchley remarks, "Andrea Brady and others that I have asked raise the important point, with which I concur, that there may be a dearth of women writing experimentally in Britain to begin with (especially compared with America). Again, this would seem down to historical and environmental conditions that have excluded women, or put them off being part of this scene, until very recently. The cliquishness and vocal dominance of men at past poetry readings surely repelled some from even attempting to be part of such a collective, not only because of the peculiar mix of sociability and self-promotion such events demand and indeed rely on (marginal to mainstream culture as they are) but also 'because it was implicitly made clear [...women] weren't welcome' as Robert Hampson has suggested (in an email to the UK poetry list, 26 Sept 2006)." Alternatively, Monk avers that this dearth comes not from male poets' conduct but "just because there weren't that many women interested in experimentation" and suggests several reasons for this.

Notably these "historical and environmental conditions" include the fact that the preponderance of publishers of non-Mainstream works and organizers of events by their poets have been men, yet in recent years this has begun to change. In 2006 Critchley organized the Contemporary Experimental Women's Poetry Festival at Cambridge, and in 2008, Zoë Skoulding took over editorship of *Poetry Wales* and has since broadened the magazine's scope. Brady founded Archive of the Now in 2005, a text- and audio-based online collection of poetry "committed to supporting non-mainstream poetry which may be excluded from similar projects."[6] Reality Street Editions, a merger of Wendy Mulford's Street Editions and Ken Edwards' Reality Studios, maintains its commitment to the publication of women's poetries, best known in this regard for its 1996 anthology *Out of Everywhere: Linguistically Innovative Poetries by Women in North America and the UK,* edited by Maggie O'Sullivan. In addition, *Damn the Caesars*[7] and Shearsman Books have publicly declared their desire to receive—and so to publish—more work by women.

Toward this end, it is important to keep our understanding of the range of Other poetries as broad as possible. Other should not simply replace "avant garde" or "experimental"; it should cast beyond those exhausted categories. As Caroline Bergvall remarked at the London launch of the *Journal of British and Irish Innovative Poetry* last year, "Can one hope that this is also opening the door for the recognition and study of poetic forms that have hitherto had an erratic, marginalized presence within English. I'm thinking here about the expanded poetics that have emerged for the past say, twenty years and that are radically redefining the terms by which poetics overall will function. Some call it 'expanded writing', 'literary arts', 'performance writing', 'performative writing', 'off-page writing', etc. They are inseparable from the changing writing, publishing and dissemination modes through which we're encountering text in social culture."[8] Other poetries—no, *poetry*— should be as inclusive as possible.

This anthology does not purport to provide a balanced representation of recent Other poetries by women born, or resident in, the UK, so much as the best such work available. Solicitations to the admirable O'Sullivan and Monk, already widely anthologized, were respectfully denied, on account of the focus on women and the desire not to be categorized; a few other requests for work were ignored altogether.

This anthology does, however, provide a vibrant snapshot at a time of burgeoning poetic activity. Five of the twenty-five contributors (arranged in this volume by age) have yet to bring out their first full-length poetry collections, while another five have only published one. This is an exciting time for women's Other poetries in the UK, an advance it is hoped this anthology will further.

For advice, assistance, and in some cases emotional support, thanks go to Andrea Brady, Matt Bryden, Claire Crowther, Ken Edwards, Robert Hampson, Sophie Mayer, Richard Price, Scott Thurston, Catherine Wagner, and the Pussipo listserv. Editor and publisher Tony Frazer has devoted innumerable hours to this project, and for that I am most grateful.

Carrie Etter
Bradford on Avon, England
February 2010

Notes

[1] My use of the word Other to denote a range of non-Mainstream poetries, while similar to Richard Caddel's and Peter Quartermain's use of the word in the introduction to their anthology, *Other: British and Irish Poetry Since 1970* (Hanover, NH & London: Wesleyan University Press, 1999), does not suppose those Other poetries as necessarily oppositional.

[2] Recent winners of significant American prizes, who would not be considered as belonging to the Mainstream, include Fanny Howe, 2009 winner of The Poetry Foundation's Ruth Lilly Poetry Prize, Nathaniel Mackey, 2006 winner of the National Book Award in Poetry, Keith Waldrop, 2009 winner of the National Book Award in Poetry, Alice Notley, 2007 winner of the Academy of American Poets' Lenore Marshall Poetry Prize—et cetera.

[3] As the editors of Reality Street Editions and Shearsman Books attest.

[4] Eva Salzman and Amy Wack, eds. *Women's Work: Modern Women Poets Writing in English* (Bridgend: Seren Books, 2008). See also Juliana Spahr and Stephanie Young, "Numbers Trouble," *Chicago Review* 53:2/3 (88–111), which focuses on the situation in the United States.

[5] http://jacketmagazine.com/34/wagner-forum.shtml Accessed 10 January 2010.

[6] http://www.archiveofthenow.com Accessed 11 January 2010.

[7] While situated in the US, *Damn the Caesars* has maintained a steady interest in Other British poetries. On the problem of receiving submissions from women poets, see the entry for November 20, 2007, titled 'Considering the Body Count'; http://damnthecaesars.blogspot.com/2007_11_01_archive.html

[8] http://www.scribd.com/doc/22924473/Journal-of-British-and-Irish-Innovative-Poetry-Birkbeck-Launch-Event-2009-Selected-Papers, page 21. Accessed 10 January 2010.

Infinite Difference

ISOBEL ARMSTRONG

A Lyric Poet? What is that? I was going to write, 'I am a lyric poet' but the question emerged almost simultaneously with the statement. Now remote from lyres and things, what use is it to call a poem by a word that encompasses anything from Shakespeare's sonnets to Maggie O'Sullivan's 'Murmur'?

But this word still retains the vestiges of 'singing'—the body used as a vocal instrument, print imprinted with the body's effort. I want to write poems of this order.

I want to say what I think I do rather than produce the binaries do/ don't.

I love Browning's words, 'I touched a thought'. They sum up the philosophical lyric that stretches from Blake and Shelley through the Rossettis and Emily Dickinson, the two women, lovers, who called themselves 'Michael Field', Hardy, Yeats, Allen Fisher, Maggie O'Sullivan, to name a few. There is a tradition of impassioned philosophical lyric that I'd like to belong to and develop. I want to find the cadences of a thought in the body.

Collage I use a lot, it comes to me almost without thinking. It's a way of making another lyric out of others' lyrics, using resources in common—a way of moving out to other people's work. It isn't just 'mine'.

I am fascinated by glass. I am writing a glass symphony. One of the themes is *Kristallnacht*.

Defining Deaths

1

the trees' past is alight

incandescing in cell and fibre

      blazing veins and capillaries

      squander aura

      the year's store of sun

leaves weightless

      time falls radiant

light's afterlife flares from the ground

        2

winter-hard tulips sealed in alabaster

yield stone to membrane

         petal-tense skin

gives   peels   pulls open

         grease-creased white-puckered

         crepuscular tissue

give themselves over to opening

      hollow out the glossy air

      afloat in air they hollow

intransigent green stems

      sinuous to water now

            give

After Iraq: reflections on a train

England's green and

Green to the very

blanched sky   traverses
        the   azure   one
the pines print   across   fleet
        sudden green pain in hedgerows
   print pain   across   green
windowscape crossings fleet window in
    adiaphane   green in

   reveries stretch across fields linked
to their dreamers   revenants
   of the retina's memories
write over   over write
           grassgreen blood in glass
blanch traces something grates in
  sandgrains greened by pineprints
     painprints glazed
      sandgrains grazed
       desert in glass

Second Desert Collages

ONE: John C. Van Dyke out of John C. Van Dyke

The Desert is Overwhelmingly Silent

mountain and mesa dissolve into
a land of fire
no food   no grass   no

water salt-poisoned   sun blood
sulphureous sublimity   splintered
peaks torn valleys   skies far-off fires   withering
sands drifting   gather gather gather
grain by grain   barren rock epitomize power
opal and topaz kingdom of sun-fire   flame
flame sovereign

Wasted upon the Aboriginal Retina

the name of nobody's hills   print
of a deer's hoof in stone   what of the footprints of
the Caesar's?   survival Nature has been
wearing away   a flat-headed man of stupidity for
an ancestor   the red man does not see
a coloured shadow wasted upon the aboriginal retina
but the cross still shines
teeth barb thorn jaw paw   struggle
the Anglo Saxon insists   only one truth
only

Almost Formless Masses of Colour and Light

illusions and thin air
truth is deceptive   mirage
over the mesa   the misshapen image
inverted   hanging in the air
we see him
where he is not
reality and phantom both appear
in the air
the snap-shot of your camera
does not catch it at all

TWO: Gertrude Bell out of Gertrude Bell

Roofless, Defenceless, Without Possessions

the voice of the wind   no life   no flowers   bare stalks bare hills
      stony road
Jordan Valley evil yellow blotched with
grey-white salt   enmity to life
winter sunset swell and fall   fall and swell
the desert breathed quietly under the glittering night
every stone the ghost of a hearth   desert dawn
waking in the heart of an opal
Jebel Druze black volcanic stones   a skyline of black stones
lava some terror petrified   frontiers of death
guards a dead land from an unpeopled

Boiled Water for me from Camp to Camp

the first gossip of the desert   blood feud camel lifting   I wept for joy
Yusef's wife no one sees
a stray shepherd standing over his flock with a long barrelled rifle
innumerable swarms of flies   there is no end to war in the desert
the days of the Belka Arabs are numbered   the mark on the ground
where the tent was pitched   the plain is covered with places wherein
      I rested
Arabs do not speak of desert   to them it is a mother country
sufficient for   the raid   a man weeping by a tent pole
questioned me why Europeans looked for inscriptions
murmur of faint voices from out the limbo of the forgotten

By Four O Clock I was Lodged in the Hotel Victoria

The Arak bottle Mikhail's fatal drawback   the riff raff of Syria
      tourist's Arabs
base-born stock half bred with negro slaves   the Turkish soldiery
in rags   their boots dropping off   half starved
'please God I shall go to America' all over Syria   a Druze

answered me in purest Yankee   you bet, so long
war the only industry the desert knows and the only game
innocuous popping of rifles   amusement without much bloodshed
men and women afflicted with ulcers and sores   children crippled
    from birth
the unmeasured wisdom of the West may find them a remedy
you stand aghast

Third Desert Collages

Out of Van Dyke out of Van Dyke and Bell out of Bell

The Voice of the Wind

overwhelmingly silent mountain and mesa dissolve
a land of fire   no food no grass   no
life no flowers   bare stalks   bare hills blotched with grey-white salt
water   poisoned sun blood   torn valleys   sands
swell and fall   fall and swell   breathed
gather gather gather grain by grain   power
waking in the heart of an opal
of opal and topaz kingdom of sun-fire   sovereign
a skyline of black stones
guards a dead land from an unpeopled

What of the Footprints of the Caesar's?

the name of nobody's hills   print
of a deer's hoof in stone   a stray shepherd
standing over his flock with a long barrelled rifle
there is no end to war in the desert
the red man does see   not a coloured shadow
— the mark on the ground where the tent was pitched
a man weeping by a tent pole   Arabs do not speak of desert
Europeans looked for inscriptions

teeth barb thorn jaw paw   struggle
the Anglo Saxon insists   only one truth

Mirage

the misshapen image   inverted   hanging in the air
we see him
where he is not
the riff raff   base-born stock   the soldiery   boots dropping off
        half starved
men and women afflicted with ulcers and sores
children crippled from birth
'Please God I shall go to America'
the snap-shot of your camera
does not catch it at all
you stand aghast

Fourth Desert Collages

Out of Bell and van Dyke Collage
1
sands swell and fall   fall and swell   breathed
waking in the heart of an opal
gather gather gather   grain by grain

a man weeping by a tent pole
water poisoned   sun blood   torn valleys
there is no end to war in the desert
half starved men and women afflicted with ulcers and sores

teeth barb thorn jaw paw struggle
only one truth
you stand aghast
the snap-shot of your camera
does not catch it at all

2
sands
waking
gather
weeping
blood
no end
men
struggle
truth
aghast
snap-shot
catch it

3

sands   weeping   men   shot   shot   men   weeping   sands

❖

Isobel Armstrong has published poetry periodically in little magazines throughout her working life as a teacher of poetry and academic. Most recently her poems have been published in *Navis, Tears in the Fence,* and *Shearsman.* A poem in *New Writing* 6, 'No-ing', was translated into Italian by Matilde Angelone and Annalisa Bergantino, who added a short interview, in *Artepresente – L'Uomo, Il Ttempo, La Storia,* NS 1, 2001, 23-26. In 2007 Equipage published a long poem, *Desert Collages.* The poems she writes are very much in continuity with her academic publications (she was Professor of English at Birkbeck until 2002), particularly *The Radical Aesthetic* (Oxford & Malden, MA: Blackwell, 2000), and most recently *Victorian Glassworlds: Glass Culture and the Imagination* (Oxford: Oxford University Press, 2008). In both these works she experimented with collages as a mode of criticism.

CARLYLE REEDY

I have not pursued the way of language which speaks of poetics of today in a language. The language that interests me is what comes through my awareness of reality, coupled with a realm of synaesthesia, an inclusion of the relationship of one kind of energy to another.

My 'poetics' of ten years ago had a great deal to do with open-field rhythms in space to allow words to convey two or three events within one event due to the placement of phrases on the page, which can often be read in clusters as easily as linearly.

I have very little way of describing just what it is I am doing in my new writing, which has come after getting past the end of the viability of looking at the world in a pure observational devotion to clarity. Much of my work was very carefully honed and considered and reconsidered before I would recognize it had gathered the most succinct and accurate form, the one the experience demanded.

The contemplative strength, along with awareness of the music of sounds and syllables and their meanings, would carefully reduce pointless addenda, in order to get straight through to the experience of standing somewhere observing something.

I do not lack patience now for such work. Much of that way of organizing sound and image in reference to the open field of the page became second nature. But since the production of a small book for Etruscan Books, which was an attempt to continue a dialogue with a poet and friend who had died, I fell silent for a number of years, producing a few poems which seemed to write themselves after doing some research—as in a poem about Afghanistan. I researched what the country and produce were in the 1930s because, having seen the landscape torn up by war, and bleak in the images that flooded the news, I wanted to get closer to the life of the land, to make a positive celebration, a paean of praise and revivification.

The wealth within that poem was a key note in a transition to my present writing. There is a fervency about translating from within the organism and its sensory apparatus a recognition of the truth of life and the intense destructivity of abstracted systems. There is a drive and a passion within me for this work. Therefore it is less intent on lucidity, very interested in chaos, extremely aware of women and children and the various people who do not make war and are caught in the midst of it, perhaps more preoccupied with that than with achievements divorced from that awareness.

To the Margin

Bring yr mind back from overpowerance, pinch
Hard if you think her heart has stopped, and rub
The smallest finger of the victim — —
That little pinkie represents ether. Hurry.

It is said to be   quick in china   that rats
With red eyes eat up your shoes as these stick out
From a blast or a stiff death. On rice paper
Where there is no photograph,   the prisoner
Can subsist   some while on the rice paper.

Dragon shape trajectories of energy
Reflect in all the metals,
In black tar, the sheen before
She died, recalling the woman
Outside in her slip, urn overturned, busted,
As water rushes a pipe, she stares
At blue flowers. Is her
Light wrap a drawing of form,
A material so soft it issues upward,
As her life pours down into the bleak pull
Of the pandemonium of the drain

She has left her birds of stiff wood pegs
on a line under the slap of vine
in the pale ironwork of the legs
of a table in what was a garden where
She appears   to recall detail

On a gamut in small maths of change
Several notes on a stave   follow rain
Into where droplets reach
For autumn and change.

They had thought to live together,
One thing, one sun, one moon
Appearing in one smile
With more knowledge than books,
A sight of themselves in light,

A touch each of each's fingers of silk,
Musics of words in pauses of death,
In a taste of old roses
Just to live, that's all, merely

Moving Thighs like leaf of banyan
Sex fruits in the long sun
Warm where she and he and she chooses
Being neither hers nor yours nor mortal
In the flight of a bird, calling them clay

Their figures dancing
In a room of allures,
Where banners of crimson wrap bodies in blood
And her live flesh dances alone forever

Egyptian, transcendent,
Hypnotic.

A bone of the body reaches far,
Making song in its hollow of rot of dust,
What knows us best
Is nature.
It Isolates and frees us.

On a board with a nail
By a window broken, big rubble
Drops and dives into a falling carpet,
The ceiling cracked in
Water and plaster,
Coming into fire.

A temporary shelter
Here or over there, the friend
You missed, did not see the bomb drop,
The burnt plastic bits, the sediment chemical of hair,

As night kept on travelling, twisting towards futures
In several incidents hurried forward faster
And fear ruled even the common objects
Yes, the room turned.

The bluest lotus is slowly going
Into oblivion in the certain process of
Nil meaning blue, utpala, Sanskrit,
Photography lurks outside the moon skin of silver birch
Wetly slick over
Iridescent snakeskin
Or human blue guts, writhing towards a solid dark,
Bloodshed turns into precious blood stone.
Dragging a veil of web, a corpse's smile
Beguiles the lone clay digger, scooping form
Around the body form until all of form is
Heavy sinking.

Chord consolations in Beethoven sinew
Continue inside the silent scream, inside a beat,
In soft packed, loose loop, millions of bright lassos
Twisting in a discarded mat thrown out by the blast
Where once did children rub bare feet to engender
Blue sparks, in laughter, blue sparkles, in light.

At a point, optimism
Sold in accents in several languages
Told a song of a chef, the best
Directing nurture and plants
From each culture in transplants, yes

A few hours, when fresh, the time it takes to
make a salad, the global nation
one world on its own home planet
In even a patch of street, where in great confusion
a star from somewhere else has fallen.

Survivre

i

On spring grasses, on bright orange floors,
On white rugs and mountainsides,
In grey pebbles, in mud of a ditch,
In times of pure water, transformations
To skid into translucent materials not of this
Planet she hopes. We are surmise and conjecture
She prays, but we might stand up.

The Skies are so pale with smoke
In the Rain, such perfect spears;
We hurry the dynamic and blast out
Even the remaining unfurling banners of grey
Omniscient asphalt, to get ahead, kill.

ii

Some sit hoping, when bombs come
They find each other's buds of tongues
So   when the order is final   they pray
Explosions seek them last, that they may
Sit side by each, watching planes like ibises,
And take of lees of wines that sink
Slowly into the mouth so speech
Becomes an iris --that all will resolve itself
In one kiss . . .

iii

Stones and snows and stains
Are on the very names of souls as
Sorrows in the wind,
Blowing over and over again
Where all were last aware.

The tree's lace is lost cloth,
For their clothing was taken.
Sun's glint is gold from teeth
Torn from mouths . . .
The earth   their comforter
      Kept together some bones,
Sinews were formed into violins,
Cellos, harps, harpsichords,
Zither strings, extending to grand pianos,
Conductor's batons, the cultural celebrations
Of silent musicians of my song.

iv

One gives another a pot of stoneware
"You will not be broken,"
The key is   old, I give the key, there will be
Trees, bushes, flowers, on land for farming
For my love does farm.
We will live in a cabin of wood on no road
Only land and land   in far surrounds.

"If I had the key, I'd put it into
one of Bob's pots, narrow necked with a wide base,
dark like the very earth.
My key will be ornate and impractical,
A kind of brass filigree . . . we would . . . we could . . .

❖

Carlyle Reedy was born in Virginia, USA, in 1938, and graduated from high school in Paris, after which she returned to the US to take a degree in Music and French Literature at Tulane University, New Orleans. After a couple of years working in New York in the early 60s, she returned to Paris, where she studied music and painting.

At the age of 19, she began working with collage, and took up writing poetry. In 1963–4 she attended London's Royal Academy of Art as a guest student; she continued writing and painting, and giving readings of her poetry in cafés and music venues. In 1967 she set up The Arts and Community Centre, Notting Hill, creating programmes of avant-garde music and theatre. After this, her work became increasingly performance-oriented, with music and visual aspects equally as important as text-based work. Her work has appeared in numerous small magazines over the years, and her many books include *Sculpted in this World* (London: Bluff Books, 1979), *The Orange Notebook* (London: Reality Studios, 1984), and *Obituaries & Celebrations* (London: WordsWorth Books, 1995). Her work has also featured in a number of anthologies including *Children of Albion, Out of Everywhere, The Virago Book of Love Poetry* and *Twentieth Century British & Irish Poetry.*

WENDY MULFORD

The best introduction to my work overall is Jeremy Hooker's article in *Swansea Review* (no. 22, 2003, ed. Glyn Pursglove). The description quoted by Hooker, of a poetry that works with conscious and unconscious elements to produce meaning that can not be reappropriated into the discourse of the known, which comes in fact from an early article in Michelene Wandor's *On Gender and Writing* (1983), still seems to me, to some extent, valid.

I do not believe my work is difficult—the difficulties in syntax and/or linguistic choices, tropes, disruption, paradox/contradiction/erasion derive from the difficulty of catching the complexity of perception and the feeling-thought complex, accurately, and swiftly, as these are always coming and going.

The poem selected here was composed for performance at the Arnolfini Gallery, in a festival celebrating the anniversary of Black Mountain College, and its associated artists and poets (December 2006). The accompanying footnotes to the ongoing I CHINA AM piece have already been transformed and are in the process of continuing change. The whole piece is absolutely a work in progress.

One of my techniques is to treat a text as theme, and play, until I tire of them, with its potential variants. The original text comes from a number of sources, but particularly from the catalogue to the Royal Academy's Chinese exhibition, 'The Three Emperors'.

The potential variations arise in the unconscious and come into consciousness as I glance through the words on the page or screen but I prefer to compose on the page, and edit on screen.

Sometimes the machine creates its own laws. Of spacing, and of marks.

Each page brings new juxtapositions, new memories, new trails, by the collision, elision or buffing of words and spaces. SPACE is equally a significant register—that which registers meaning as well as sound, part of the orchestration of the poem.

I CHINA AM

i

longevity speaks

                                    fragile you

                                                        entered

seal   script unfolded

                                    an underslip

a waterway

                        leading

                                              nowhere

baffles

                              ripe

                                              pomegranate

jade

               [d]

                         linghzi

                  solitary   salute

★★★

        I China am

                 silent presence   am

brushing the silk

                 inside   your elbow

how

        an ear-lobe hangs

Bodhisattva

               a cartouche

                              bronze bodies?

to exchange in the

                    Heavenly Kingdom

female   I unfurl the

                      Underworld

each mark the

                 hawk hangs

the

        body-map

              turquoise

slays my universe

            led

                    blessings the

dragon bestowed for

                  tranquillity restored

shorn from the

            lacquered halls

flames stepping & the

                  Mother of God

            prays

★★★

floating silk

        pellucid screens

                yield to

military guise

        wounds   the scholar

poet

        incomplete knowledge

                broken

science

        wisdom bodes slant

                shapes the

shaman's skull

        or a wandering monk

who is revealed

        you need to know for

blue vessels likely

           limn the horizon

what matters yearning

           for trackless

              journeys

show

        the stupid inkstone

              stability's a

monochrome

        events   opening

upon a

      habit of

        not hearing

as the words   run out

★★★

ii

the heart

        the underworld

                each marks

the place is it

        me speaking   can you

colour that dragon who's

                strayed into

the universe scoops

          blessings tucked

into the nine

        fuck

           tranquillity's

fetched up

        Whooo

              flares happiness

which day   which

        night   which moon

the Jesuits floss

        smile a

              possible

self designs the

        floating   silk

             reliant

upon

        the stars and

          heavenly courses

if the scholar

        poet   strays

           come back

the Altars of Earth

        yellow, red, blue

Commence

            INKSTONE apply

                     the

    lifetime   habit to

                         open up

   the scroll

            of the Dead

                    review

Perfect Brightness

                  revivify

    ceramic

           porcelain

               stone

                  shall signify

the New Year's

           observance

                 a

one-handed

           furrow

                   then

             ★★★

the instructions

           elsewhere

                   rises

very ancient

           ancestors   bamboo

               flute

             cranes

are offering

           the surround is

ruby

           peach

                 the robe officially

in the place of

                    the fire-eater

Auspicious

               remember in the

                           Palace

perfection attends each

                     brush-stroke

    else the

               orders awry

                         blessed

raider and the

                    fire-clawed

    reliquary

              relinquish

                     your hold

no more

              world   ruler

iii

Only the hound
            brushing past
                       keenly
scents
      the last
                restless
                     that's
deposited
            innumerable
                   hangings
seals
           calligraphics   the
                  virtuous
ambition's trove
              store's recollection
believe otherwise
             the fragile
fisherman's raft what's
               organic
                  decays

are you tempted
           to be assiduous
turn aside
        from borrowed music
chimes
      bells
           dogmatic treatise
jewelled movement
              the erstwhile
monuments
        of the literati
     so many shades of
          silence

✧

Wendy Mulford grew up and was educated in Wales, read Archaeology and Anthropology and English at Cambridge; after research, writing and a lifetime teaching, in all manner of institutions, escaped from London and Cambridge to a village near the east coast where she has lived for 20 years.

Since 1977 she has published 13 volumes of poetry, 2 works of non-fiction and edited *The Virago Book of Love Poetry*. Wendy Mulford ran Street Editions (later Reality Street Editions), which she founded in 1972, for 26 years. Recent publications include *and suddenly, supposing: Selected Poems* (Buckfastleigh: etruscan books, 2002) and *The Land Between* (Hastings: Reality Street Editions, 2009).

CLAIRE CROWTHER

Though this selection may not specially represent this, to me the art of poetry is most fulfilled by line. Shaping, sorting, clumping and cutting line—making connected words give far more than the individual words could be so that they are almost abstract sets—this is what satisfies me. I give poems different lineations depending on content and context. I like to use line as the primary way to manage the development of meaning through a poem, like a ladder. Poems are just word ladders, really. For example, even a prose stanza within otherwise lineated stanzas can represent a change of foothold within the poem. What form should not do, and this is why I usually avoid traditional form, is mask what I think of as my perceptual dyslexia. I don't readily understand the usual narratives. I accept them, I can work within them—I have to work within them—but don't understand much of them. When I write a poem, I use line to uncover and climb over the lack, rather than the fact, of connection within an accepted syntax. I am interested in what we think we are doing as much as what we are doing. My poetry has been called fractured, strange, nonsensical. To me, it's simply a word-equivalent of an unlined world, as sturdy as I can make it.

Young Woman with Scythe

As if soil was noise, the legal notice
shivered on the barrow. Louise tore off
her scything gloves. High on a pine, wild
parakeets, harbingers of change
in our climate, stared from their margin, chattered
about apocalypse. Carefully, eking
out a holiday, I watered plants.
That's my dialect of territory
against the elocution of possession.
I looked for so long at Louise's face,
that, in the bedroom mirror, it smoothed mine.

A Seafront Wake for the Postwar

The ruin on the island keeps away fragmented steps,
shoulder bone of upper storey arch, lady chapel, rank
of skinned arms cracked at the wrist.

New houses creep near like animals listening to the old—
Teach Me Tonight—magnified through a trumpet
fixed to the mother-board.

My time was blonde scraped up in a froth. Now our white hair
is arranged against purple. From birth, the agenda of regeneration
confuses us. 'Skip It.'

I read future time by Attlee as surely as if those clock hands beamed
on the wake wall from a light disguised as a camera are snapping
facts. All of it is skin

though now it shakes loose of flesh, once stock still like rock inside.
An old man's hands flick his horsetail metres.
The wind turbines rush round.

'Pat's been a Samaritan since July.' 'My new man's got a boat.'
Sea gatefolds each page of wave and tears.
The Struggle is Over.

Books (A Friend I Had)

Books love dust they wear it like skin my friend
Wouldn't say I'd betrayed her (she's alcoholic
She gets up early with glass hands shouts interrupts

Business conversations forgets she has phoned
Her texts are illegible as though her predictive
Can't understand her) I have a library of meat eaters

Predatory words (to give her up with as a matter
Of long course not paying attention drop
A call drop a card) meanwhile a library warms

Itself in blood even if it doesn't hunt (what
Did she do wrong the statues were hidden beside
A yew she dragged them into prominence

One has no arms and yet holds a snake she needs
To learn some interested faces but gave up
Birds any reference to the despised species

The blue tits the dunnocks we ran home in the late-
Victorian blanket of houses between my estate
And hers down Olton Hollow round Greycourt Crescent

Through Castle Lane against the orange painted dark
Heels hammering toes bleeding) the tickle tickle
Of animal voices and tree tops trying to get in

Once Troublesome

'Let them call her a wicked old woman! She knew she was no such thing.'
—Vita Sackville-West, 'All Passion Spent'

It isn't New Year yet so Happy *What?*
Till then, it's Boxing Day every morning.
Empty bags hang off the radiators.
Chilly: hot
          cold
                    Cordelia position.
          Did it mean
we didn't love each other
that morning he gave me up
though that same night he said, *Let's marry?*
      My striped dress hung
             along my body
                bounced
            boldened
           bitmapped
my abdomen as I walked, a balloon
        sinking back down
           its own string
      after the decision.
The baby would have had to sleep in a drawer.
            Immortalists
(not you who refuse to believe improbable notions)
think:
      the smallest cell refuses to die
      in its everness.
Now I live in an attic
garden is the chewed melon skin of sky.
Old bins, old books. Death's hardly ethical
in the light of such continuity. Last week,
the CEO of a charity named in my will
wrote to suggest ways to retrieve what I've lost.
Look, Christmas photos
      of others' other
         children. After
           Pocoyo, Juggling Balls.

❖

Claire Crowther has published two collections of poetry, *Stretch of Closures* (Exeter: Shearsman Books, 2007), *The Clockwork Gift* (Shearsman Books, 2009) and a pamphlet, *The Glass Harmonica* (Pilton: Flarestack, 2003). *Stretch of Closures* was shortlisted for the Aldeburgh Best First Collection prize. Her reviews and poems have appeared in a variety of journals including *Poetry Wales, New Welsh Review, Poetry London* and *The Times Literary Supplement*. She has a PhD and MPhil in Creative Writing (poetry) from Kingston and Glamorgan University respectively, and won the Shakespeare prize and the George Gissing prize while studying as an undergraduate at Manchester University.

DENISE RILEY

The poem, as Williams put it, is a machine, and a feeling-machine at that. Editing your poem can seem like finishing off some small vehicle's bodywork: aligning, spraying, patting, smoothing, after bashing the thing around. The emotions generated as it whirrs along might sometimes slow down into forms of attitudinizing. Hence the first title here, 'Rhetorical.'

My attempts at writing stay strongly attached to lyric, and to a continuing modern lyric, its cadence and musicality, and its meditative powers. Merleau-Ponty's helpful observation—that we are not wholly enclosed in our separateness but are outside ourselves from the start and open to the world—is one I've often had occasion to draw on. The second of my editor's selections here, 'Outside from the start', reflects on this while it runs through its thoughts about song, and the petrification or the stiffening of song.

Rhetorical

To be air or a black streak on air, or be silt.
Be any watery sheen threading brackish, or vein
nets tracked as patted under their skin glaze, running all ways.

Cascade of stubs.
Buttercup metal glow, ruff of dark strawberry tulle
in any vehement colour night you get blown into hundreds.

Is that clear as a glass stem cups its chill in its own throat.
Is it true that candour so tightens the integument of the heart
that quartz needles shower from the cut mouth of the speaker
though the voice opens to fall:

If you can see me, look away
but swallow me into you

And I must trust that need is held in common, as I think it my duty to.
That every down-draught's thick with stiffening feathers
with rustlings from pallor throats
as the air hangs with its free light and its dead weight equally

'Outside from the start'

i

What does the hard look do to what it sees?
Pull beauty out of it, or stare it in? Slippery

heart on legs clops into the boiling swirl as
a pale calm page shoots up, opening rapidly

to say *I know*—something unskinned me, so
now it bites into me—it has skinned me alive,

I get dried from dark red to dark windspun
withered jerky, to shape handy flyports out

of my lattice, or pulled out am membranes
arched bluish, webby, staked out to twang

or am mouthslick of chewed gum, dragged
in a tearing tent, flopped to a raggy soft sag.

Yet none have hard real edges, since each one
is rightly spilled over, from the start of her life.

How long do I pretend to be all of us.
Will you come in out of that air now.

ii

Black shadows, sharp scattered green
sunlit in lime, in acid leaves.

Hot leaves, veined with the sun
draining the watcher's look of all colour

so a dark film moves over her sight.
Then the trees glow with inside light.

Hold to the thought if it can shine
straight through a dream of failed eyes sliding

to the wristwatch's face, wet under its glass
a thickening red meniscus tilting across its dial.

iii

And then my ears get full of someone's teeth again
as someone's tongue

as brown and flexible as a young giraffe's
rasps all round someone else's story—

a glow of light that wavers and collapses
in a *phttt* of forgiving what's indifferent to it:

not the being worked mechanically but the stare
to catch just what it's doing to you—

there's the revulsion point, puffs up a screen
tacks cushiony lips on a face-shaped gap

a-fuzz with a hair corona, its mouth a navel
not quiet, and disappointing as adult chocolate—

I'd rather stalk as upright as a gang of arrows
clattering a trolley down the aisles

though only the breastbone stone
the fair strung weltering

a softening seashore clay
steel-blue with crimps of early history

the piney trees their green afire
a deep light bubbling to grey

long birds honking across
the scrub, the ruffled shore

coral beaks dab at froth
the pinched sedge shirring

unbroken moor, spinney rushes
petticoat brine, bladderwrack-brown

coppice rustlers, always a one to fall
for—Cut it, blank pennywort charm, or

punch of now that rips the tireless air
or gorgeous finger-stroke of grime.

iv

True sweetness must fan out to find its end
but tied off from its object it will swell—

lumping across sterile air it counts itself
lonely and brave. At once it festers. Why shape

these sentiments, prosecution witnesses, in violet
washes of light where rock cascades to water bluer

than powdering hopes of home. A hook's tossed out
across one shoulder to snag on to any tufts of thrift:

Have I spoken only when things have hardened?
But wouldn't the fact of you melt a watch?

Unfurls no father-car umbrella here. No beautiful
fate is sought, nor any cut-out heart renunciation

—if only some Aztec god could get placated! But he don't—
there's just a swollen modesty to champ at its own breast.

High on itself, it sings of its own end, rejoicing
that this cannot come about. Because I am alive here.

v

The muscled waves reared up, and scrupulously
no hints of mock neutrality were lost.

Containment-led indifference, or conspiracy
accounts of generals' pensions, cost

no setback for the partners of democracy
who portioned barnyards out to each *volost*

while florid in the twilight, Nation stood
alight above the low dismembered good.

❖

Denise Riley is currently A.D. White Professor-at-Large at Cornell University, and was Professor of Literature with Philosophy at the University of East Anglia. Books include *War in the Nursery: Theories of the Child and Mother* (London: Virago Press, 1983); *'Am I that Name?' Feminism and the Category of Women in History* (London: Palgrave Macmillan, 1988); *The Words of Selves: Identification, Solidarity, Irony* (Palo Alto, CA: Stanford University Press, 2000); *The Force of Language*, with Jean-Jacques Lecercle (London: Palgrave Macmillan, 2004); and *Impersonal Passion: Language As Affect* (Durham, NC: Duke University Press, 2005). She also published *Penguin Modern Poets 10,* with Douglas Oliver and Iain Sinclair (London: Penguin Books, 1996), and *Denise Riley: Selected Poems* (London: Reality Street Editions, 2000), and she edited *Poets on Writing: Britain, 1970–1991* (London: Macmillan, 1992) and co-edited *The Language, Discourse, Society Reader* (London: Palgrave Macmillan, 2004). She was formerly Writer in Residence at the Tate Gallery, London. Recent work studies philosophies of self-presence, the neurophenomenology of self-awareness, and the history of understandings of inner speech and how these enter into our ideas of what's interior and what's outside.

FRANCES PRESLEY

Some of my recent work has been concerned with issues of translation, inheritance and experimental poetics. 'Learning Letters' is based on a Dutch primer, 'Lezen leren', that I was given in the 1950s. The primer is influenced by its original co-existence and co-publication in colonial Dutch Indonesia. I was the lazy learner, when English was always enough. I did not learn my mother's tongue properly, although it is as familiar to me as English, perhaps more familiar as an ambience, an atmosphere, a sound.

Movement of 'o', or the 'oo', of my uncles. This language of double vowels, as if one vowel were not enough. What is the effect of this extra vowel? I am searching through the empty vowel, through so much loss, but also the 'oo' of the present indicative, the language of indicators, of pointers, of delight, of light through vowels. Correspondence from Eric Dickens: "There used to be more written long vowels in the 19th century, but since the spelling reforms they've economised by knocking out some of them, while still retaining the long sound."

Learning to recognise their sound, their shape on the page, and their colour. A limited number of colours can be used in the book: orange is one of them, which is appropriate for the House of Orange. "The two colours, orange and turquoise, are perfect complementaries and together produce 'white'. The after image results from areas of the retina becoming desensitized to orange and turquoise because you have stared at the picture for so long."

There are echoes in this poem of a conversation with Hans Thill, and his harpo-poems *Kühle Religionen* (Heidelberg: Verlag Das Wunder-horn, 2003), as well as Johan de Wit's *Monkey and Tiger* (London: Kater Murr 2004). I was also involved in the co-translation of Paul van Ostaijen's long modernist poem 'Bezette Stad', organised by Karlien van den Beukel and Elizabeth James. Van Ostaijen's text presents a linguistic challenge, and experiments visually, partly inspired by books from his childhood. I am rediscovering children's books with the help of India, Miranda and Alina, and I am working on an alphabet sequence with their father, the artist Peterjon Skelt.

Learning Letters

My first book for the first year of learning

Published by P. Noordhoff N.V. – 1953 – Groningen–Djakarta
24th impression, pressure of letters
erste druk, first struck 1919

Lezen leren, to read, gather, glean   lazy learner   graze

oo

the boys are saying oo from behind a bush
saying boo to a goose who is only their uncle

oo   –   oo   –   oo   –   **oom** !

swinging his stick which could be his cane
in the bachelor life of busby berkeley
                a new formation

oo,   m.
        m.
        m.

it's still an o that ends in an m

in german it's ohm
ohmic and resistant in this electrical current

oh!

uncle

oh,   u.

u.
u.

were always the silent kees

        aa

oo . aa . oo . aa . m.

    the uncle's cane is pointing to his name
    hanging from hooks in the shop window
    and what's an ape doing here?
    the ape is also pointing to its name

        aap

    he thought I said arp or harp, not ape
    harpo
    the problem of sound
    reducing itself

    the monkey is a pointer
    will take the cane
    become the cane
    hanuman

oo . oom . aa . aap.

    the monocle de mon oncle

    moonkey   unc

    the monkey's uncle

    ape uncle

    learn to ape, boys

    the monkey is the wit

een   eet

     learn to eat
     one eats

     in a 'kamer' or 'eetkamer'
     come eat
     an invitation
     a going in
     an openness

     an ape eats
     an orange pear

     drops a pear
     and uncle munches
     but uncle canes
     the tree and monkey flees
     dropping a pear

     eat an uncle?
     eat an ape?

       af
       a   **f**

     off
     uncle
     down

     hats off

aa   aaf

     little aaf she
     runs in on page thirteen

af, aaf

off, oof   – preferring consonants

an uncle is an oh look!
a girl is an off
or an after
thought

off on a tree
hugs
the base

the monkey is on
the monkey tree

uncle is in the under
growth

       e

e.   **e.**   **e.**
    aa   eef

eef is a baby girl
eeny
meeny
e

held by aaf
fed a pear by orange
haired aaf
aaf eats and
eef eats

e   **n**

eef and aaf
aaf and eef

and   and   and

i

who is in
who is in the onion?
on the onion
round the onion
round and round

uncle
eat the onion

     ik

ik was always stronger than i

ik stands more firmly on the ground
asserts what it does and doesn't know
is crisp with k

h/ ic and familiarly me

when did we lose the i who was both consonant and vowel?

ik   ook.

not i

oh, uncle, me too. me too.
    me up, and eef down.

    me too
    brother
    not to be left
    off

this is the girls' favourite story

me too! me too! **me** too!

louder on each succeeding page

       r

r.   **r.**   **r.**

    is an air on a rattle and not available in our tongue

    it was available through the tongue which i can roll

    wanting to hear and arrr and ear and veer and ere

    and err and oar

    and o'er and roar

        an ear on an uncle

        an ear on an onion

    an orange ear

          an ear on an ape

    an ear on aaf

            so

             off

s   s

      s.   s.   s.

FROM ALPHABET FOR ALINA

a

apple a pull a tree a lina
leans her aap pull an apple an
ape sun ap rise across a cross be
tween cox and box her sunset keep
her kept such red to last such red to read

a tart start heart wood this year
the sun gone set or unripe apples
for supermarkets not my favourite
checks to come and live in caravans
pays less than factory work leaf eaters

whose apples who eats this
apple do not snow white do not
white out my reading burst let her
breathe let her choose between apple
and mirror of the apple her s/own character

Frances Presley was born in Derbyshire in 1952, and grew up in Lincolnshire and Somerset. She now lives and works in London. Publications of poems and prose include *The Sex of Art* (Twickenham & Wakefield: North and South, 1988), *Hula Hoop* (London: Other Press, 1993), *Linocut* (London: Oasis Books, 1997), and *Private writings: a Vermont journal* (Exeter: Maquette Press, 1998). She collaborated with artist Irma Irsara, in a multi-media performance about the fashion trade in London, *Automatic Cross Stitch* (Other Press, 2000); and with Elizabeth James in an email text and performance, *Neither the One Nor the Other* (London: Form Books, 1999). *Somerset Letters* (Oasis Books, 2002), with drawings by Ian Robinson, explored intersections of community and landscape. The title sequence of *Paravane: new and selected poems, 1996–2003* (Cambridge: Salt Publishing, 2004) is a response to 9/11. *Myne: new and selected poems and prose, 1976–2006* (Exeter: Shearsman Books, 2006) includes two landscape sequences: the most recent is 'Stone settings', an approach to the Neolithic sites on Exmoor, which is also a collaboration and multi-media performance with Tilla Brading. This reappears with further new work in her most recent book, *Lines of sight* (Shearsman Books, 2009). Presley has also co-translated the work of the Norwegian poets Hanne Bramness (*Salt on the eye*, Shearsman Books, 2007) and Lars Amund Vaage (*Outside the Institution. Selected Poems*, Shearsman Books, 2010).

CATHERINE HALES

I think the necessity of poetry is to irritate, to evoke the uncomfortable response. Scraps of language from different places and registers—radio, tv, conversations, lawyer-speak, etc.—coalesce and collide, creating meaning from their juxtaposition, meaning that is not subject to control or definition but (among other things including just being what it is) questions the rules by which we are obliged to live, like grammar, syntax, meaning. Look in vain for (linear) narrative, for anecdote, for epiphanies, for messages, for making-the-world-a-better-place: the world is a mess and language is messy and the world is language and any attempt to tidy it up with poetry is falsification. There is no utopian vision—utopias tend to end in concentration camps and piles of skulls. Putting the poem into something resembling conventional form is thus supremely ironic. It's like putting the genie back into the lamp. I like the subversive possibilities inherent in the tension between the fact of the poem as form, as an object on the page, and its necessary conceptual rejection of form; the irony implicit in calling a fourteen-line poem a sonnet, for example. At the same time, form gives meaning somewhere to start from. If something then stirs beyond and behind the words and if that something is glimpsed but cannot be grasped, like a smudge of smoke on the horizon, and if some people choose to believe that that something is akin to what they choose with imaginative shortcoming to call god, then so be it. I prefer to call it image in something like the Poundian sense.

Yes, it all started with Pound, with his Dos and Don'ts, and with Eliot's 'Waste Land'; but also with Sylvia Plath and Brian Patten and Adrian Henri and the *Children of Albion*. Peter Dent has probably been the biggest single influence and nurture. It took a long time for the poetry I write to get approximately to where I could start publishing it. Every poem is still a surprise; if I knew where a poem was going before I wrote it, I wouldn't write it, would I?

divination

signs   drenched in meaning   early
dew   and another fine   but maybe

later cloud   shudders like a headache
lightning   it'll pass   where

were we then   ah yes   the signs
we were seeking   the words to tell

than venice

by the waters of   sofas empty bottles plastic bags full of
with a skinful of myself I just like to walk on my own if that's

the shriek of swifts dropping through air &
the photographer starts by painting the model's body

the archaeological record's real   all our mythology's
ariel awol & caliban in his soul   stale bread &

small pools caught in fists of petals   disposal
fronts propelled by trenches of pressure   accumulating

until she's invisible against the brickwork   all this at my
take another look at   yes & some of it lands in the

context

the clarity of the thought   present
tense   where were the water gods when

we needed them   still & translucent
perfectly packaged residue of artefacts

nor plagued with notions of propriety
paralysed   the splash obfuscated by its

sudden contingency   allowing her at least
the veracity of a slingback   wanton

hooves across halogen flora   the arch-
aeological record is real   it can't lie she said

divergences

to be among them   the red buildings
red brick in the sinking light   & in them

rooms glowing gold in reflected light
from wooden floors   uncluttered white walls

a winter's gravity   & dispassion   as of
equations proving a parallel universe

brushing my cheek with its wind   or that I can cup
in my hand and toss   but never see   only mind

can conceive   when freezing may well happen
wind scissor in from the arctic   snow deaden

across the

singularities out there sucking light   so many
laid the foundation for a face-to-face

grinding millet   lighting fires   the tip of the mountain
outrageous to award a free kick for   where did I hear

a shopping mall is now a lifestyle center
the woman walked out into the water weighted

from the window we could see rising from a bed of cloud
its beam marking the sands   if we set out now

waves increasing frequency   he went supernova
deep into the present   mint   crushed cumin

from f/5.6

3.   the fence   *for yisha*

the price of a large-format photo   the ex-
hibition toasted in the press   & with a
champagne opening   corporate take-
over of a near-death experience   the way
she told it   iron-tipped or stones
caught in the grooves of the rubber
profile   dusty & with a splash of
could be blood   the insoluble problem
walled off & none may approach
or enter the restricted zone   when
the border guards raise their smgs
she said   you run   the first
thing a photographer needs   she said
is a good pair of boots

❖

Catherine Hales grew up near the Thames in Surrey and, after a few years in Norwich and Stuttgart, now lives near the Spree in Berlin, where she works as a freelance translator. Her poetry and translations of contemporary German poetry have appeared in many magazines, including *Shearsman, Tears in the Fence, Poetry Salzburg Review, Fire, Stride, Haiku Quarterly, Great Works* and *Shadowtrain*. She is a co-organiser of Poetry Hearings, the Berlin festival of English-language poetry, and has been described, by *ExBerliner* magazine, as a "Berlin poetry heavyweight". She has published two pamphlets, *out of mind* (Berlin: flash pamphlets, 2006), and *a bestiary of so[nne][r]ts* (Old Hunstanton: Oystercatcher Press, 2010); *hazard or fall* (Exeter: Shearsman Books, 2010) was her first full collection.

Anne Blonstein

Notarikon and gematria:
from Hebrew hermeneutics to personalized poetic procedures

Notarikon and gematria are rabbinical methods used to interpret the Hebrew scriptures. Since 2001 I have been appropriating and adapting these methods for the writing of poetic sequences.

Notarikon might be viewed as a form of reverse acronym. Each letter of a word is perceived as the (usually) initial letter of another word, to thus expand the original word into a phrase (i.e. a 5-letter word becomes a 5-word phrase). I first applied this procedure (in *correspondence with nobody*) to Paul Celan's translations into German of 21 Shakespeare sonnets. The first word of Celan's translations is "Was" [What/That which]—which in my notarikon became the first (and perhaps programmatic) sentence of the book: "words and silences".

After *worked on screen* (written in 2002)—whose source texts were the titles of 108 artworks by Paul Klee—I too focused my attention on (parts of) the Hebrew bible. Various decisions have to be made before the writing can begin. First and foremost, how to "convert" the Hebrew into the Roman alphabet, since there is no one-to-one correspondence between them. In each of the four sequences I have written so far, the choices were slightly different. When writing such pieces, I also have to bear in mind that most readers will have no familiarity with Hebrew and will not recognize the source words that have given the notarikon.

The 66 poems of *and my smile will be yellow* (five of which are published here) incorporate at their end (in "des lèvres closes", also at the close of the first stanza) notarikon of just a few words from successive chapters of Isaiah. Even if the Hebrew original remains occulted, moving through the sequence, the reader will notice certain repetitions with variation. For example an "i.../y... hands v.../w... hows" phrase occurs eight times and is a notarikon of the Tetragrammaton (יהוה), the (unspoken) name of God.

In *and my smile will be yellow*, along with notarikon I also used gematria for the first time. For gematria, the numerical values assigned to the Hebrew letters are summed to give a total for each word. This is used by Jewish scholars to identify e.g. otherwise unmarked equivalences between words or phrases. I apply it somewhat differently. The gematria value of a word yields for me in advance the spacing to be incorporated in and around the notarikon phrase; i.e. in addition to generating words, words also engender gaps, breaks, lacunae ...

You follow me into the shadowed room

where *a story is told* · *and yet there is hardly any real narrative*
structure | *there are no answers* · *they would sabotage*
the speculative gesture of what is being told · dreamt
and rhythmed | *as if i had heard clouds* · *snow* ·
sound gravitations · *shadows* | engratituded |
and subjected from these
inner chambers : choices begun in a
random assortment of shadowing
nows hows | variations on an identity in one . . .
exercised on an inner keyboard | a corpus of beginnings
to cite a language (housed)

Notes
Title: Barbara Guest: Storytelling. *The American Poetry Review*, Sept/Oct 2005,Vol. 34 /
No. 5, p. 53

a story is . . . Alfred Zimmerlin: Akrobatik und Groteske. «Musica» in Strassburg —
eine Momentaufnahme. *Neue Zürcher Zeitung*, 4 October 2005, No. 231, p. 44

there are no . . . Martin Krumbholz: Bin ich's, bin ich nicht? Gert Loschutz' Roman
«Dunkle Gesellschaft». *Neue Zürcher Zeitung*, 4 October 2005, No. 231, p. 43

as if i . . . Raphael Urweider: Musik hören. *Neue Zürcher Zeitung*, 1/2 October 2005,
No. 229, p. 68

Isaiah 1: 26

hell–nicht–ausgelöschtem

answers are more difficult than questions | her dress rippled
with the untolds | *and we live in this rabid capitalism · terrible* |
and so she bought thirty-six candles | *the realization is full
of accidents* | maroon and ash–grey and gold | strolling
the arcanes | in an interrogation of yells lost irreplaces
logistics . . .

no wounded stories of faces vanished . . .
into torture | legal fantasies and logic justifying
the torture
(me here alone · the winter there . . . it's
mine . . . night | cold | solitude)
white links of shame are ruptures indices
of torture ?

Title: 'bright-not-erased'. Boškvo Tomaševič: *Celan trifft H. und C. in Todtnauberg.* Aus dem Serbischen übersetzt von Helmut Weinberger. Berlin, Das Arsenal, 2005, p. 25

answers are more . . . Aimé Césaire in an interview with Marion Van Renterghem. *Le Monde,* 16 December 2005, p. 20

and we live . . . Giovanna Marini in an interview with Patrick Labesse. *Le Monde,* 16 December 2005, p. 29

the realization is . . . Pierre Boulez: *Leçons de musique.* Paris, Christian Bourgois, 2005, p.74

Isaiah 15: 2 & 9

Dort wo die Nähe bleibt,

where repairs to a paradigm | "i feel you close to me" |
exercise books filled with notes in which the refugees
describe their difficulties — *the cold* · *the lack of food*
| *the work* · *in turn* · *has no precise moment of origin* |
personal letters · *diplomas* · *torn passports* | for producing
clear discriptions | a cheek ... nightwinged ... flew
into irreversible memories

anchorless in a shadow-river — a beetle zigzagged
across   ancient whisperings
alphabetical looseness — most quite   in a whore's
mouth   :"show me —   your hands   a whereness
of hows   "

Title: 'There where the closeness remains'. Boškvo Tomašević, ibid., p. 56

exercise books filled . . . personal letters . . . Cécile Hennion: Egypte: 'L'évacuation forcée
de réfugiés soudanais tourne à la tragédie'. *Le Monde*, 1–2 January 2006, p. 6

the work . . . John Benton: 778. Roland dies at Roncevaux. Entering the date. In: Denis
Hollier (ed.): *A New History of French Literature.* Cambridge, MA, Harvard University
Press, 1989, p. 6

Isaiah 18: 1, 2 & 7

syntax is a faculty of the soul | they had worn ballgowns to the funeral
· crushed pale-grey silk · chiffon · they had cried · and in their faces
scoured inside to translucency she recognized ·   · the angels
of her ancestors | discuss the limits of surtainability |

                                                              | exit visas   :

                              | love in extendable vistas

                                                        | exile visas   :

                   | love in expressible viscera |

                                        | quarrel with

                   | love as a quotable value |

                                   | quoted when

                   lovers quarrel   in winter |

"night was falling as i descended to sit beside your shadow | a
              wet night   shapes blurred into real visitors
         whose nights lamented   chanced   a darker welcome

into diasporas of bare rhythm — your hands   waltzless
                                                             hows"

Title: 'of closed lips'. Francis Giauque: *Œuvres*. Vevey, Éditions de l'Aire, 2005, p. 49

syntax is a . . . Peter Szondi in Christoph König: *Engführungen: Peter Szondi und die Literatur. Marbachermagazin* 108, 2004, p. 5

Isaiah 28: 13 & 14

und ich geh'

to speak a language one has never learned · she wore a black linen
coat · at least three generations too large · so she could reach into
hidden pockets · to · rappen for street musicians · lemons ·
a kingfisher's flight | for lovers they had only
reflections | a volume of nettled-greek lessons
(windprinted) |
volumes of charred letters — exclusively bound
in amniotic membranes
a volume   champagne-natured . . .: a blast of lectinned tears |
or the white curve on black ground · that they called thought

mandateless in an open language — sought   found
read . . .

Title: 'and I go'. Selma Meerbaum-Eisinger: Abend II. In: *Ich bin in Sehnsucht eingehüllt.*
Gedichte. Herausgegeben von Jürgen Serke. Hamburg, Hoffmann und Campe, 2005,
p.42

to speak a . . . Eva Almassy: 'Dromomanie et glossolalie'. *Le Monde des livres*, 17 March
2006, p.2

Isaiah 34: 4 & 16

❖

anne blonstein: born 22 april 1958 in harpenden, hertfordshire. great-granddaughter of jewish immigrants. moved 1966 to cobham, 1975 to guildford, surrey. 1976–1979: degree in natural sciences, selwyn college cambridge. 1979–1982: plant breeding and genetics doctorate, cambridge. 1982–1991: post-doctoral cell biology research, basel, switzerland. father died 1986. mother died 1988. 1991–1992 read dickinson, h.d., bishop, plath, rich, howe and howe . . . 1992–1995: copy editor, karger verlag, basel. since 1996: freelance translator and editor, basel. books: *the blue pearl* (cambridge: salt publishing, 2003); *worked on screen* (salzburg: poetry salzburg, 2005); *memory's morning* (exeter: shearsman books, 2008); *correspondence with nobody* (basel: ellectrique press, 2008); *the butterflies and the burnings* (basel: dusie press, 2009). since 1999: regular collaborations with the swiss composer mela meierhans.

ANNA RECKIN

As I look at the selection here, I'm very struck by how many of the poems connect with the visual arts. 'Notes', for example, had its origins in an artist's book project where a number of poets were asked to contribute pieces to appear on sets of wooden cubes strung on wires. Our poems thus exist both as individual entities, published in two dimensions, on paper, and as dynamic elements in three-dimensional abacus-like collaborative 'books'. 'Fabric' is one of a suite of poems written in response to 'Chasing Mother's Lace', a series of artworks by Joan Woods based on manipulated photographs of folded textiles.

I think it's the experience of opening up to multidimensionality—which also draws me to writing about landscape—that makes visual art such a powerful element in my writing. Much though I love and admire the British canon, and a fair amount of the British and American so-called mainstream, I'd given up on writing poems of my own until, in my mid-thirties, I got to see a completely different kind of poetry, in graduate school in the US. Here, for the first time, I was exposed to poems full of gaps and edges, poems that were porous and scary and which seemed to me to have a kind of direct, intimate, playful, risky relationship with poetry's basic materials—words and sound, space and duration—that I instantly recognized. Mei-mei Berssenbrugge and Myung Mi Kim were visitors to the programme. I had a week at Naropa with Kathleen Fraser, started to read Robert Duncan and Susan Howe, Kamau Brathwaite, Lyn Hejinian, Barbara Guest, Cecilia Vicuña, Ronald Johnson. I do believe poems can change lives. Duncan's 'Often I Am Permitted' did that for me.

Although I rarely, if ever, write the expressive lyric of feminine self-determination, that impulse is nonetheless a driving force in my poetics. In my writing I'm looking and listening for poems that direct attention to the best kind of attention I can pay to words and the way they work in the world—for good and for bad. It feels a very personal, particular task, and at the same time utterly open, unbounded, detached.

As if that way

Move in amongst, as if

that way

you could hear

these grave-

posts, groves of gums,

dots of tree-shade:

       stems to be lost and listening in,

       between 'here stands,' under

       stood-for's

set foot, and scatter

   stet

     – as if it could

Based on *Edge of the Trees*, an installation by Fiona Foley and Janet Laurence at the Museum of Sydney

Still-room

       as moss: grease and powdered dark

           fields in jars.

      iris, rose, herbs   fixture & loss

           water's hungers

                  fleet as grass

Fabric

dusk   shoulders   ivies   bride's

name-tag   hips   girdle   blossom

folding   *figured*   *forced*   *repeats*

[ ]   satin   tartan

                           poppets

                [parition   ]

Lone Thorn

Flicker of folklore, mazy as a March weather-vane. Barbed wire, tangles; how quickly sex smells like decay. It's that fining to a point I have a problem with – splitting the thread, draggling the tension. Sparks and crackles, dissipated power. Durst not gather, nor gather round, nor deck with rags

Poor shall, poor may, poor Martha Ray

notes

points

lawn-spun star

fine- tuning

much
  darker,

  much cooler

  mote's
  hung

cross-hair

❖

Anna Reckin made a career in publishing in England before going to graduate school in the US, where she took an MFA in Creative Writing at the University of Minnesota and then a PhD in the Poetics Programme at SUNY Buffalo. She now lives in Norwich, where she teaches part-time for the University of East Anglia's Centre for Continuing Education and follows her research interests in landscape and experimental Anglophone poetry. Her poetry has appeared in magazines in the UK and the US, including *Shearsman, How2* and *Chain*. Her first book, *Broder* (Minneapolis: Traffic Street Press, 2000), an artist's-book collaboration with photographer Paulette Myers-Rich, won a Minnesota Book award; a pamphlet, *Spill* (Buffalo, NY: Chibcha Press), appeared in 2004.

ELISABETH BLETSOE

A missal contains the text and often the music to conduct the Christian Mass throughout the year and the one at Sherborne was created c. 1400 for the monks of the Benedictine Abbey there. It is unique for its remarkable marginal series of naturalistic birds, most of which are native to the area and given their dialect names. Studying and writing about the birds allowed me to explore my favourite themes. I observed each bird in its real habitat around Sherborne or its outlying villages and then linked it back to the missal by means of religious iconography, imagery relating to books, pigments or methods of illumination and bird mythology, the latter often subverting the original Christian intention. I employed my version of the Japanese haibun as the roughly similar-sized blocks of text looked pleasing to me on the page and the haiku allowed for a brief word-sketch of the bird itself to literally "illuminate" the whole.

Birds from the Sherborne Missal

I.
Unnamed, identified as Goldfinch *(Carduelis carduelis)*
for Suzanne

Days of brief transparency, viewed through a window of ice, lifted. Powdered across the lane. Having a porous cuttle texture as if drawn "using a thin & rather scratchy nib". A stricter regimen being currently observed, blood temporarily withdraws. Lenthay Copse smokily obscure. Brittle scrapiness of reeds, bones packed tight with air. Fish-spine delicate. A tenebrous rustle, like the breathing of books. Fields growing nothing but stones, bone white, buff white, ivory white, carved by the river Yeo, formerly the Gifle or forked one. Abounding in small flocks among the alders; a *c'irm* or charm indicating a tinnitus of small bells, blended, a continual weaving of waters. Angel speaks with multitudinous voice. "Thistle-tweaker", a conflation of thorns with the scarlet forehead becomes the iconography of crucifixion myth, ousting earlier fertile goddess affinities. Its nest a vaginal metaphor; a labyrinth of tender intricacies. *Lucina*, caged by the fingers of holy infants.

> sparkling up from
> the dried burdock heads, "a shrill
> piping of plenty"

II.
Roddok, Robin *(Erithacus rubecula)*

Becoming secretive & depressed in the later months, before the vigorous reassertion of autumn territory. Stakes & ties. Paths of observance newly laid through contusions of aster, sedum & verbena *bonariensis*, helmeted with bees; offertories yielding a roman tessera, three pebbles from Chesil Bank & a tennis ball. A smell of burning moxa. Sulphur being ground with mercury to form vermilion; glazed with madder, sealed. Red as a releaser (your fat cherry lips), the impossible fury of it all. Oscillograph of the throat, that bob bob bobbing thing. Boundaries constructed from scribbles of sound. Marginals encompass the crossing at North Road, where fifteen burials "very shallow & without coffins" marked the putative site of Swithun's chapel. Haunter of low places & diggings, befitting associations with early resurrection cults. A bird so hallowed such that, harming it, the offending hand would forever uncontrollably tremble. Bringer of fire from the chthonian levels, that our lives might blaze inches from shadow; burnt feathers colour of bright fame. Covering the bodies of the dead with leaves.

> tweezing grey hairs
> in the bathroom; outside a robin's
> winter song

III.
Unnamed, identified as Woodcock *(Scolopax rusticola)*

Being considered as late as the eighteenth century that they spent their months of absence on the moon, an idea preferred to the risible new migration theory. The declension from lunar pastures, a glissade down streams of refrigerant light congealing while filtered through earth's atmosphere. A millenial count of sixteen on the Sherborne estate recorded as "noteworthy". Frost-triggered, tumbled by Siberian winds; a fall, falling. Into daylight hours of trance-like stillness. Lines of infection tracing the foundations of the derelict war hospital. The isolation unit, brambled. Aggregates of hyphae form underground cities of mycelia; endless ramifications, the deliquescence of fruiting bodies. Earth pigments, superfine ochres, sepia & sootblack in a complex marbling. Almost present, not quite absent; *I am not here, I am something else.* Limned in such manuscripts owing to the succulence of their flesh; whole, roasted. Hepatic lobes of beefsteak polypore exude a sanguineous juice; votive gifts pressed into bark fissures: sheepwool, calcite chips, a palm cross, attended by wasps. The pin-feather sought for its precision fineness "to remove the mote from thy brother's eye"; mounted in silver, to bring a woman to pleasure.

                    in my mind's
            eye, brooding, a heap of dead
            leaves on dead leaves

IV.
Stare, Starling *(Sturnus vulgaris)*

Ring-angels on the radar testament to starling diaspora. From the Greek, *psaros*, spotted or flecked. Hand against sky leaking through fingers; the point where everything breaks through. Refractive famishings. Flight as a single-celled animal, a granular flow into pseudopodia, pushing towards fission & fusion. The twisting of nuclei form trace-memories of divinatory meaning. Pound Road; domed canopy of the Monterey cypress, gravid with song, counterpointed by five flute-towers of Lombardy poplar in Blacksmith's Lane. Sugar of hedge-fruits turning to alcohol. Rumours of adolescent sciamachy; the stoning of hanging baskets, toppling of garden urns. Attempted gun-sales at Pack Monday fair; addicts buying lemons at local stores. The passage of saints-days in a watershine shatter of glass: Wulfsin & Aldhelm, Emerenciana & Juthware. Rough music, *charivari*. Ammoniac stench of the roost inviting various scatological nicknames. (Shitlegs). That petrol iridescence. A breast, "crowded with lustrous stars".

                    blackberry theft;
                juveniles mimic Richard the
                    cabbie's ring-tones

V.
Waysteter, Pied Wagtail *(Motacilla alba)*

Ambiguities of black and white. Delighting in even a small & temporary gathering of waters. In brief fugue through the osseous bird-cage of the monks' lavatorium; an emersion of helical patternings under the rain glaze on its blue liassic floor, star-creatures lost in chalk seas in primordial times. Elemental scratchings; refusal of the public-school boys to tread its deep surface, architectural spaces infested with elegant & obsolete ritual. Ancestral games. A sylph-like buoyancy against the cohesive bulk of the abbey, internal voices transmitting its prescriptive fictions. Darkening ghosts pasted to the weighted song of the stone, damply. A conduit, to lead, but nowhere, of the emotions; lengths being taken to avoid extremes, the careful monitoring of lithium in the veins. Unwitting bride, squaring up to the lens under Bow Arch, place of rebel execution. A veil escaping in a stirring of winds; a bird in lovely & undulant motion. Carrying within, always, the leaven of instant flight, the announcing of wings.

> running running   shaking off
> three drops of devil's blood from the tail
> > tip

VI.
Mew, Gull (family *Laridae*)

Moving into the more solemn part of the Mass; gold foil running through the hedge, buffed by a wolf's tooth. Clifton Maubank, *Clistune*, concealed by dark flickerings of holly-oak; the storm horizon. Walled about with a batteled wall & "sette with all sorts". With naked foot stalking in my chamber. Legendary ash plantings, the once ever-open door. The writhe of negotiations & giftings. Alluvial soils, prone to flood: in fallow waves bathing, broading out their feathers among small flowering crucifers crushed by the hooves of cattle. Lustral gatherings; the flock a lucent stillness, heart's needle fixed to the south-east. *Varium et mutabile*, the cupreous light. A driveway, chagrined by leaves, pinnate & palmate. Breaking within, stone by stone, piece by piece, the structures of desire; the sun's low deception. Resteth here, that quick could never rest, *laros*, the ravening ones, implacable spirits of the drowned. An absent finial, a tree hairy with virus. The last worst enemy, to face impermanence; sunlight flash in a seagull's wingpit.

"Sea-gulls, winter mews,
haunt the fallow.
Beetles flie."

VII.
Sparwe, Sparrow *(Passer domesticus)*
for Michell

Waiting for Sylvia, who never arrived. In back of *The Plume of Feathers*, a narrow sanctum in hibernal state, graced by the fluttering of small lives. Mimosa racemes. Roof-angles, at variance, drawn by the impetus of the abbey tower against ever finer & finer grindings of lapis & azurite. Into depthless sky. An insistent cheeping surpasses the bells' doxology; illicit couplings betrayed in a tremor of ivy. Naked stems of the winterstruck clematis proximate to the red bench, a simple narrative that becomes more complex; there is you, myself & many others like fingerprints among the lichen, staining. Faces that open & close. Things half-buried, annealed by frost. The inn a former mortuary, museum of autoptic secrets; no random event the disclosure of a statue of the risen Christ hidden within its walls. Sparrows gather, conductors of souls; only one human pair of eyes witnesses the child riding her trike across the flagstones. Back & forth, back & forth.

high gothic letters
blown by the wind; let sparrows
make a nest of them

VIII.
Heyrun, Heron *(Ardea cinerea)*

A page that encompasses the whole sky folds down to the shape of a heron, flying. Avian blood-cells a reliquary from cretaceous days; the serpentine throat, the gist of reptiles. Pterodactylar span devouring land gifted by Athelstan as barter for the soul's yearly mass; to Aenna's Pool, the Coombe of the Pigsty, Ecgulf's Tree, Aetta's Dean, "for all time".

Pastures garlanded with wire & electricity. Barbed & tanged. Bird flesh that waxes & wanes in lunar synchrony with the lady's smock, vacillatory cress-hordes at the margins of the parish water-meadow. *Fons limpidus.* River-ephemera gather at Smear's Bridge; pollen spicules, florets of eltrot, a meniscoid bulging. The circumspect gaze; irides chrome-yellow, orbits naked, livid. From the banks of the Yeo, a stone frieze of three Magi, one bearing apparently a head, severed. A boy bringing to school a heron killed while attempting to swallow a live vole; the children of Bradford Abbas being "deeply interested in this riverside tragedy".

> water glancing light;
> the long patience

IX.
Throstil cok, male Blackbird *(Turdus merula)*

Desultory & melodious with more intricate phraseology as the season advances; discarded notes upwardly forming invisible rooms of ancillary miracles in which to inhabit/yet to be built. Song-post on the Almshouse roof a nodal point above the facial ruin of a luetic angel. Imperatives from the Lamb & the Eagle. Reciting of our Lady Psalter five times daily in contemplation of death & judgement, a cloister of swept shadows. Trendle Street, Westbury; abandoned on unassuming corners, the simulacrum pertains. Teenagers dressed in rags of birds crowd the doorway of Docherty's Bar with aromas of batter & pea-wet. Distinctions elide between male & female, dark & light: [overheard] *"I'm in a state of flux right now"*. Apprehensions of subcutaneous violence like a distant bruise, a sky staining with orpiment. Budding yeasty moon under poriferous cloud. A saint opens a hand to find in his palm a small blue-green egg. Words thicken, unimportant & unanswered. Only being alive is left; the pulse, tic of raised tail-feathers on landing. Sung for its own sake.

> midnight alarm-calls:
> last bird of evening or
> first of morning?

❖

Elisabeth Bletsoe was born in 1960 at West Parley near Wimborne in Dorset. She has degrees in psychology and history and once worked as a post-graduate tutor at Cardiff University, while also leading adult education courses in women's studies and creative writing. Her works include *The Regardians* (Nether Stowey: Odyssey Poets Press, 1993), *Portraits of the Artist's Sister* (Odyssey Poets Press, 1994), *Pharmacopoeia* (Nedther Stowey & Plymouth: Odyssey Poets + Terrible Work, 1999) and *Landscape from a Dream* (Exeter: Shearsman Books, 2008); the first three books have this year been collected by Shearsman Books into a single volume entitled *Pharmacopœia & Early Selected Works*. She guest-edited '*Odyssey* 20: Unanchored in Ecumenopolis' (1996), appeared in the anthologies *Earth Ascending* (Exeter: Stride, 1997), *The New Exeter Book of Riddles* (London: Enitharmon, 1999) and *Don't Start Me Talking* (Cambridge: Salt Publishing, 2007), and has been broadcast on Resonance FM and Radio 3's *The Verb*. Since 1997 she has lived back in Dorset and is involved with administration, conservation and research at Sherborne Museum. A lifelong student of plants and plant medicines, she is currently writing a biographical book on a little-known female botanical artist, Diana Ruth Wilson.

CAROLINE BERGVALL

Cropper exists in two versions ('2006' and '2008'). Each version pursues with a slightly different emphasis the development of an autobiographic structure. Through it the text outlines a number of artistic processes and thoughts about poetics. In a sense, I was (especially in this 2006 version) trying to summarise my motivation for making work, that part of it that deals with language use and its embodied ramifications, what it means to have a body full of language/s. Verbal and semiotic pleasure always has its hard pendant; language as an invasive and disturbing intimacy, structured by rules that implement inextricable control over our bodily and mental perceptions. For the rhythmic core of the piece, I developed interjections in Norwegian. These interjections connect up and intercept the main body of the piece, turning it into a bilingual structure, inflecting the English in the process by creating, in a final instance, a new syntax for the piece. Indeed, in Norwegian, "som" is a conjunction used to introduce relative sentences or sub-clauses. This interweaving of rhythms and languages (known or unknown to the reader) seeks to dynamise and transform the work's modality, by giving it a push from personalised poetic account to public address.

Cropper *(Kropper)* (2006)

Under pressure my hands sometimes balloon to the size of small waterbombs, now that I've been travelling across 8 time-zones, and haven't slept in 26 hours, or haven't slept in 3 months, ever since I started working at an invitation for the second 06 issue of *Nypoesi* and the invitation had read or haven't slept in 8 months for many mysterious reasons, please write a piece in Norwegian—

    noe i noen

Taking the bissextile leap year into account, and imagining that I started on January 3rd, I've been developing for the past 89 days, we're April 2nd, a complicated network of pages designed to stage or otherwise demonstrate my sense and senses as a diasporic Norwegian poet, although strictly speaking I'm not diasporic, or rather so in an ambiguous free-to-roam White European fashion since I wasn't forced by circumstance, this being debatable at a psychological level, but made the choice, chose to write in English, ever since I no longer could write in French, being acutely caught up, caught too acutely in its le-la structure, and having not so far developed work in Norwegian, yet both languages had initially shaped one's physical and mental outpost, my linguistic physiognomy—

    noen i noe

Now I look in my shelves for a book on the bilingual brain by Suzanne Romaine, a British sociolinguist who contends that born bilinguals develop resource allocation not brain damage, a different physiological brain and different cognitive responses from monolinguals and from those whose bilingualism takes place after having first acquired one language, but it must be in one of the boxes I still have in New York where I spent most of last year for I cant find it—

    noe en finner i noe

My journey across was not traumatic, from Paris to Oslo to London with corresponding passports, the gaps appear not at entry, only with the passing years, I had immediately taken to London's queer sensibilities and enjoyment of iconoclastic performance traditions, and the city had seemed to take to mine, absorb me into her, under railway arches, on the stages of late-night clubs in flamboyant and revamped South London pubs, in the rooms of local performing arts venues, in strange claustrophobic poetry rooms—

nå som en er kroppslig

When one arrives to language fully grown it's fair to think, isn't it fair to think that one's past bodyshape can be left blissfully in the dark, that one can start at a new one, yet perhaps one should have imagined that this body would lack most of the somatic and cultural presumptions familiar to standard bearers of a language and a country where daffodils are not so much spring flowers as wandering clouds, indeed how reliable was this light-headed roaming, a state of cultural aphasia, and would one have to learn to embed the nursery rhymes, the cultural undercurrents and scaffoldings to sounds and sense, create a developing infancy, a 3D spec of my shape and skin, or could one simply forego this one and carry on from a poetic imaginary eerily free of white rabbits, split instead between Norwegian trolls and French childhood songs about bridges and ladies in medieval gardens—

som en stadig er

How does one keep one's body as one's own, what does this mean but the relative safety of boundaries, could I make sure that what I called my body would remain in the transit from other languages, that it would hold its progression into English, and because I didn't know and wasn't sure, and since for a great number of people, for an overwhelming number of persons, for an overwhelmingly large number of persons, for an always growing number of persons, this is far from self–evident, this is not self–evident, this is impossible, this does not apply, this doesn't even begin to figure, I never knew for sure—

som står for noe som står for noen

Some never had a body to call their own before it was taken away—

*som hadde aldri en kropp de kunne kalle sin egen før den ble
revet bort*

Some never had a chance to feel a body as their own before it was taken
away—

*som fikk aldri oppleve en kropp som sin egen før den ble
revet bort*

Some never had a chance to know their body before it was taken
away—

som fikk aldri kjenne sin kropp før den ble revet bort

Some were never free to speak their body before it was taken up and
taken away—

*noen var aldri frie til å si sin kropp før den ble løftet opp og
revet bort*

Some tried their body on to pleasure in it before it was taken up beaten
violated taken away—

*som tok sin kropp på for å nyte den før den ble løftet opp
slått krenket revet bort*

Some had their body for a time then it too was taken away or parts of
it—

*som hadde sin kropp i en tid så ble den også revet bort eller
deler av den*

Some thought they had their body safely then were asked to leave it
behind the door or parts of it—

*som trodde at de trygt hadde sin kropp bare for å bli bedt
om å la den bli igjen bak døren eller deler av den*

Some hoped they had one safely only to find it had to be left across the
border or parts of it—

som håpet de trygt hadde en kropp bare for å innse at den
måtte bli igjen over grensen eller deler av den

Some wanted to leave their body behind and couldn't—

som ønsket å legge sin kropp bak seg og kunne ikke

Some could neither take it with them nor leave it behind—

som kunne verken ta den med seg eller legge den igjen

Some are laughed at some spat out some are dragged into the crowd—

som blir ledd av som spyttet ut som blir trukket inn i mengden

Some bodies are forgotten in the language compounds—

Some immense pressure is applied on to the forgetting of the ecosystems some escape from—

Some bodies like languages simply disappear—

noen kropper liksom språk blir simpelthen borte

Some or many are being disappeared—

noen eller mange er blitt borte

Some or many disappear—

noen eller mange blir borte

Some or many that disappeared arise in some or many of us—

noen eller mange som ble borte reiser seg i noen eller mange av oss

Some arise in some or many of us—

noen reiser seg i noen eller mange av oss

Some that arise in some of us arise in many of us—

noen som reiser seg i noen av oss reiser seg i mange av oss

Some that arise in some of us arrive in each of us—

noen som reiser seg i noen av oss kommer frem i hver av oss

Since words are vibrations, patterns of activity, bodies prefigured and thought out, and since colour acts as a reminder that beings and objects are vibrations, in the end but vibration, intense attraction spreading and balancing in the volume, terrible conflictual resonance at the bounds, colour perception being one of the more primitive thus grounding components of the human visual apparatus, I imagined three texts that a reader wouldn't be able to read but could perceive, three texts that would function perceptually, as perceptual texts, hand–coloured blotches, a mix of ink and coloured tint, gold leaf and colour that would force up a physical or sensory reading, a reading that would rest primarily on the experience of density and contrasts, and since according to the philosopher Irigaray, but I would need to check on this, colour remembers the womb, or an inseparate inseparable space, its knot of connections, much like language begins as a sensation of structured resonance, the texts would enhance linguistic recognition at the level of a neurological response, yet every day I am unable to complete the task—

noe rødt

I went on to imagining three visual texts, or visual patterns, each occupying a page and developed by counting and multiplying the letters of three chosen words, three Norwegian words, each chosen for their nodal effect on my personal experience of bounds, actually two substantive nouns and one Swedish name, a family name is a starting-point, organised on the page according to a strict and rigorous code, so that they could in fact be read but would by virtue of their seductive visual organisation, mostly be viewed glanced at, their visual look edging towards verbal meaning, and would favour more immediate sensory and responsive knowledges, like the work of visual artists and poets interested in the transformative aspect of hypnotic patterning as

Caroline Bergvall / 93

a release from identity that is a release into motion perception, or the work of meditation traditions that seek in the demanding refinements of repeated postures and arrangements a pathway to cultural engagement, yet every day I wake up uneasy and unable to complete the task—

noe orange

I went on to imagining three poetic pieces, to be written in English, yet I wondered whether letters from the three chosen Norwegian words might perhaps not appear bolded up in the English, and whether the dots of the i's could perhaps be gilded as an acknowledgment of the prior illuminated work, written in a dry and lyrical mode of sorts, or let's just say a mode that would allow me to call on personal events as well as on the writings of three writers, Marina Tsvetayeva, Hélène Cixous and Adrienne Rich, although in early versions, I had also wished to rely on Danielle Collobert, Reinaldo Arenas, Nazim Hikmet, twentieth century writers uninvited, unable or unwilling to function at its historical breaches, yet who did, whose function it was, and had in the end loosely settled for these three, to think about various forms of internal and external exile, two of whom alive at the time of writing, who've used their writing and writing–lives specifically in an intimately public way, to place their intellectual and poetic bodymass in such a way, as to block resist and bear witness to enforced forms of kinship, force applied to language, the eradicating forces of gender on individual and collective bodyshapes, yet every day I wake up angry and unable to complete the task—

noe gult

For three months I did this, sat at my desk, watched my hands balloon, and pondered on three perceptual texts for a physical placement and a sensory form of knowledge, three visual patterns for a reading locked into a contemplative form of structural participation, and three poetic pieces for an investment in conflictual language belongings written in the currently most globally assumed language of capital, each of these modes willing to address what it means to cross a border, a rule, a boundary, a limit, an edge, it all seemed consistent, yet every day muscles and nerves would shock me into an inexplicable procrastination, shame me with frequent incapacitating fevers, what is this inability to complete the task, these set tasks, is it a way of holding one's breath, of closing one's eyes, of looking away, of not going out, the eczema that is spreading on one's skin, under one's shirt one's clothes, invisible mostly, seems to work analogically, clogs the fibres of one's language, a literal way of showing that a body didn't just add chunks of meat on crossing the tongue, on doubling on tripling the tongue out of tyngde into noise, but a tongue's mind, the inbuilt certainty of ground, now could the deployment of tentative forms, speechless patches, memory gashes, textual prompts, be made to circumvent, even circumnavigate this fever, this skinned unease, scrape at its allergic need, scrape off the need for soil for thick for tongue, don't produce ways of slipping that are ways of slipping of choking, of choking of jumping inwardly fearfully, falling fearfully out of step, from everything and many—

noen lunde

Now unbeknownst to me, my semi-nons, these clusters or heaps of nons that make one up, or sum one up, that is until this moment, at this point of writing, stretched at the very fine end of these months of a labyrinthine activity, something had shrugged and jumped, many things point to where she left off, the motion shadow, the ripple in the air that follows the jump, had she mistaken the line for a private refuge, skin warps or wraps around injury, adjusts to some new bulk, had she been hiding, hesitating on either sides of hyphenation, had I mistaken the hyphen the dash of my cultures for a full stop, had I wished for it, to stop at it, to hide on it, no longer looking out for or following the connections, the urgent pathlines and the networks, critical forms of friendship, starshaped demand attention, public address tuned to a point of raw nerve of accentuation demands perseverance, as if one would be hyphen, seduced and lost in tales of origination, rather than declare oneself jiving on it off it, having it for a plunge, a real dive, jump from the springboard, the diving–board, a capacity for sympathy, the kind of sympathetic structure that rests on mental stimulation and physical availability, emotional discipline and open-ended shapes to drive the energy and see the sentence through, to dive in the mid of the next, and wake up mid–stream, wake up streaming, inside the skin, under the skin of her time, they are being marched off line—

noen brytes av

Caroline Bergvall is a French-Norwegian writer and artist, based in London. Her work is concerned with new literacies, multilingualism, speech and body, cultural performativity and new citizenry. She has developed books and textual pieces as well as audioworks, visual textwork, net-based pieces, live readings and sited performances, in Europe, Scandinavia and North America. She writes in English but her work frequently addresses her multilingual background. Collections of texts and performance pieces include: *Eclat* (Dartington: Sound & Language, 1996), *Goan Atom* (Cambridge: rem press, 2001), *Fig* (Cambridge: Salt Publishing, 2005), as well as the recent chapbooks *Alyson Singes* (Brooklyn, NY: Belladonna, 2008) and *Cropper* (Southampton: Torque Press, 2008) and her first Norwegian output *Plessjør* (Oslo: H Press, 2008). Recent collaborations include the sound-text installation *Say: "Parsley"* (MuKha Museum, Antwerp, 2008) and an arts residency with visual artist Rodney McMillian (Hammer Museum, Los Angeles, 2009). Also a printed matter output *The Die Is Cast* with writer Nick Thurston (York: information as material, 2009). Other presentations include Tate Modern (London), MOMA (New York), PhonoFemme (Vienna) and DIA (New York). She was the Director of Performance Writing at Dartington College of Arts and co-Chair of the MFA in Writing at Bard College. She is the recipient of an AHRC Arts Fellowship in the Creative and Performing Arts, 2007–2010. Her website is at www.carolinebergvall.com.

CAROL WATTS

Tracking the process of my work across different artforms, and through the territory of the lyric, is something I resist articulating. That resistance is important acoustically. I work with what feels like the music—or pitch—of language, the visceral sense that it calls you out, makes you ring like a tuning fork. Working in a silence, full of noise and word arrivals, frequencies, poetry takes place. A passage of writing that remains as open as I can make it in that moment to unknowing, curiosity, thought, breath. Such a calling out is social, interpellative: thinking about Denise Riley's poetics was formative for me in this regard. I'm interested in the matter poetry carries and communicates. How it disarms, alongside forms of nonrecognition and opacity that are nonetheless intimate, shared. The energies it releases: kinetic, humorous, painful. I think of poetry in part as encounter—one that at its most intense reveals the stakes of living in a world where language is technologised, shot through with administrative logics or devastating reason. As registering the cost or freight of that. And also as offering, in a space of continuous exchange with the work, thought or voices of others, a kind of joy.

'Hare' is one strand of what I do, first published in 2007. It has been read as an example of contemporary nature poetry, and I'm interested to test the limits of what that might mean in the twenty-first century, as in *Zeta Landscape*, which engages explicitly with the pastoral. 'Hare' cuts between material drawn from two places: the Welsh myth of Melangell from the Tanat Valley in Powys, and South London, where I live. The tale of a seventh-century woman who saved hares from a marauding hunt, is interleaved with the case of a murdered teenager who saw himself as a superhuman protector of his friends. His story was related in the media at the time by those who knew him at the extraordinary social project, Kids Company. The sequence sets something running: questions of protection and violence, projected fantasies of care, what social love would take.

from **Hare**

SMALL malachi from a thin country   darting through
rivulets, or as large as scree clouds looming at night
the speed telling,

only. Called up by December green, unseasonal, in long lines.
Fitting the lines the length of a span, the leap from
there under the yews,

to this place. Sudden shift, when legs are collected under,
a coil where not being is this instant of generation, pushing
out, in tensile

covenanting with the next minute. Where joy is, but in
unknowing. These small brown limbs flung far, broadcast,
followed.

Where the eye fails, and rain falls in grit pinions, it holds
you to coordinates, a hunt begins. Horns sound, alarms,
low aircraft traffic, all

drum out of thickets, skeins of light, noise beating
to send them all rising to be picked off. Do they run
even in grey places, among

pelts of road kill, the scavenging of organs. Wings
take to the air from tangled spaces. Sometimes there is singing
or lips are soldered, as if peace

arrives. Running only in dreams, or in the reveries
of motorway borders, the fields stretching like a haunch,
pursued,

is returned to the head of the stream by the lych-gate
runs to return there. But hangs in the air over isles
of dogs, a quarry and

the pace of provocation, in long alert, waiting
to set intent in motion, anticipating hills, a flow
without protection, naked, to itself.

WAKES with eyes open, as he was born, stubble
formed and seven feet before the mirror, shaves
long ears rough

as tongues, as a rasp. She or he wakes also, finds
a comfort in his form, pricked up as high as he can go,
auricular

erection, listens to voices. Deep inside that hurdy-gurdy
of a barrel chest, is a threshing box, is an engine
cranked to beat

rudely, to answer lungs. The length of his thighs
propped against the sink, does she or he span them
knowingly, or

remember the dark place, where they were last
surprised, the burr, the patches on the moon are
rank

scent rising. The point where fullness is a day shadow.
Its pearl blush, that she or he would think it vulnerable,
only to discover

with night, its beacon shining. Scalding skin,
clouds boil away, leaving in desire
she or he

precipitate. Is there a thought of husbands
in that look. Is that look the thought owned by
no-one, moving

in its own accord. Does it cut across his shoulders,
the nape and clavicles, reflected, in nocturnal
relinquishing, in quiet

release. She or he turns over, he reaches eight
feet to the tip. Looms powerfully, is deep in his
imagining.

BREATH on the heels is damp and hot, where
he skims the stream, tracking the length of a road
twisting, showers

arrive violently. Heat, and the birds scatter in blue
and copper, their heaviness dropping in the air, or
congregating, as hens

might, their cries are stones grating. Thought is not
diagonal but round, a place of cockpits. It lies low,
in daylight

equal to the land. Night rises from the peat, drummed
up, it takes uncertain routing, never alike. Whales
founder

in the meadow. Leave their rib cage behind, panting, as if
the dive takes all they have to give, needing
lightness.

Small malachi   finds a blow hole in the dusk, lifts,
is lifted. Spewed up, spins in shards and bones, sprung
as a lock

picked by uncertainties. Does remain, or takes to his limbs
leagues out, when the frenzy is upon him, though
not of his frame,

its own making. Palpitations in a beating heart, responding
to the call of anxious breezes, the inconstancy of
prediction, is

a thunder of feet pursuing. Is what excites him, sets him
a kilter, the juddering of a plate on a stone floor, it
wheels

and clatters. He streaks, to himself in the flow of things,
brown as matter, is liquid as a trick of the eye in its
instancy.

OVER underground rivers, waterlogged light of a low
sun, he strides out. She or he sees him go, watches
shadows

lengthen until. His reach is long and thin, pectorals
wasting in the day, spindles the length of the street,
reels

she or he along. Wire in the blood, nicks some inner
heart, tears it slightly. Does he lope, now, out of earshot,
wordless

greeting, sssup! from a doorway, slaps his palm. Towards
the squawk of traffic, dull interference drowns
intimate

recognisings, how do they know him. She or he sits
conjuring remonstration, steam rising from the cup.
Or is it

some extended sharing. You know his enormity
(it is really mine to see), she or he explains, I give you
permission, yet.

It is not sought. Where the land lifts, as if once,
under the concrete carapace, there was an order
of belonging,

is not the path of the river. Where the hill rises
there is no hill but is a memory of uplift, as if it sticks
in the craw,

a geometry ruminated but refusing transposition,
to be broken down, it remains to be stumbled over.
He is

a seven league animal, strides above declinations
and roots, the gouts of tarmac, that is why they
hail him.

....

STARTLED, fly up. Fog lifts, in its membranes the firs
of frost, exposed, are woody veins and stems. Heaviness
arrives,

thunder of flesh impelled, and hooves. A hunt begins,
there is always the lag of commotion, distant intention,
trumpets

try to cut to the quick. Hounds head off in some dog
turbulence. Traps are sprung, peremptory logic in the bracken
extends arrogance,

expects yews to begin growing again at its blood
instruction. Whip. Small malachi   senses the crack
before

it undulates in the air, feels his backbone ride the wave,
is off before his limbs know it. Shifts in the undertow,
evading

the love of mastery, how it cuts like a scythe. If it could cut
it would peel his pelt like a Christmas orange, leaving
whiteness,

its bitter pith. Or shave him close, docked and punished,
tossed to the scrum. Do we love rites of suffering
enough

to sport with the inconsequential. He does not know,
there is art in the abandon of him, it is all his own, voices
parrying.

Today there is a gnashing of teeth. Sweat is sleek, it makes
him dark, ringstraked, as if the wild is in dialogue. Heaviness
arrives,

he shoots and ignites, as will does. Teeth champ and chunter,
bells and bridles, abstract streaks of shouting. Is there possible
shelter.

OUT on the Rye it is dark graininess. Corpuscular light
is shiny close by, no texture to it but the gleam of wing
mirrors, beat

of strong engines, it vibrates without lenses. Skin is not multiple,
it is what is, it shakes and stutters actually. Pores are
cavernous, yet

distance is a skulking, it adjusts. Where does that glance go.
Where will it go, and what is its accounting, see him walk
by

with others, spilling out. She or he is shut off for the night, is
slumbering, to go home to. In the morning to wake also,
in

comfort and homecoming. When wings fly up they cause
consternation, the panic of expulsion from small spaces.
Catch

a beating gentle body, and release it into generous air. Does
it sleep in falling, still. Yes they do release into his strong arms,
he rocks

them gently, his brothers, they are all his kin, would he
carry them if they tired. Sometimes he is as big as
houses.

They could live there. Voices ask what do you look at, man.
Red afterseam of tail lights, unblinking shine of rain,
footsteps

running are something saved in water. Voices are high, they
break in age and reckoning, shout, making weirs and
sluices.

It is two a.m. and he feels its appointment, its regrouping.
Is it a show he has seen before, a calling out, such instinctive
voiceover.

BREAKING from the line, the cover of trees, he is run
to ground. There is only form, a hollowed out
gesture

of home, it is not enough. To stay him, the catcalls of
flying things, long languorous wings, mock in duration
contrarily, where

he is a bolt, a brown impulsion towards. Ending is unthought,
it is a simple falling, where flesh begins, in steadiness
it goes on

or it does not, even and. There is reflection in naked water,
it meets at the centre, sometimes in stillness. Where he might
enter,

on occasion. Yet he. Leaps from adjacent places, where
the clarity of contours astonishes, the length of a valley
graven

by doggedness of ice is the line he runs. Is it a keen line cut.
Ending is unthought, it is a place of imperceptible hungers
pricking

continuously, the numerousness of fog, kinds in pursuit, it lasts
as a fold persists, turning over inward. Minutes are endless
catching

in to flutes and skirting. The repetition of beating arrives,
drums up resinously, it fills the morning with boughs and
disquiets,

drags trophies behind. Trumpets fuse to mouths
in hot breath, bugles stifle, nothing calls out knowingly
while betraying.

It is not a simple falling. Small malachi   is a lamb folded
in a thin place   what remains is not a saving however
you regard it.

IS it guns they bring in urban standoffs. Tell the nature
of facing out, do they rise to seven feet of him, the affront
of ears.

They return in a hunting beyond amalgamations of childhood,
bones stretch and voices stagger in a craking of mechanical
birds,

are alarums. Sour milk, sweat of skins refracted in night
gloaming, points of cold pain rush through in the way fear
arrives

like a thorn bush. What are you doing here, man, looking. Skin
extends as the earth does, it has its curvature, the body of a mother
never

owned is a comic book salvation, heroics are her blue cloak.
At night its folds are darker, warm as a salve, you might
turn shadow,

or venture invisibly. See they are armed with voices also. Drummed
from undergrowth, the possibility of acquisition in a world
without weakness

is something to be fought for in oil and bonuses, territorial gleaming.
Gunned down. Gunned down. Is gunned down. Has been gunned
down.

Look. She or he is quieted. Now he stands unblinking as he was born,
exposed in his form, kin to himself, without community, is
cacophonous

as a crowd lifted, he spreads their assignations before him. Is it
a forcefield shouldered to tumultuous recognition, is he the greatest
wall

seen from space. Laid out, his legs are leagues. His child's feet poke
over the slab. Is he a hare loosed, chasing in long lines, does he still
want

❖

Carol Watts lives in London, where she co-directs the Birkbeck Contemporary Poetics Research Centre. Her poetry includes *brass, running* (Cambridge: Equipage, 2006), *Wrack* (Hastings: Reality Street Editions, 2007), *when blue light falls* (Old Hunstanton: Oystercatcher Press, 2008) and *this is red* (Southampton: Torque Press, 2009). Her ongoing work on prime numbers and the pastoral, *Zeta Landscape*, is published in the ecopoetics issue of *How2, Poetry Wales* and anthologised in the radical landscape poetry anthology, *The Ground Aslant* (Exeter: Shearsman Books, 2010). Visual work includes *alpha**betise***, now an e-book, and projects that move among collage, drawing and painting, and live voice/dance. A sequence told through shopping receipts, *Horrid Massacre: A Récit*, is online in part at *Ekleksographia #3*, and due out in 2010 with apple pie editions. She is currently working very slowly on an illuminated book called *O Calla*. Critical work includes *The Cultural Work of Empire: The Seven Years' War and the Imagining of the Shandean State* (Edinburgh: Edinburgh University Press, & Toronto: Toronto University Press, 2007).

ZOË SKOULDING

For some time I've been exploring the idea of the city, looking at language itself as a kind of architecture. Writing in English in the bilingual context of north Wales, I'm intensely aware of how place is multiplied by the languages that speak it into existence. However, some significant texts for me have centred on Paris, particularly Walter Benjamin's *The Arcades Project*, and also 'Formula for a New City', a situationist manifesto by Ivan Chtcheglov, published in 1958, which is a playful investigation of how the buildings and quarters of an imagined city might create different states of mind through 'an extension of psychoanalysis into architecture.' He calls for a re-visioning of the city that will restore imaginative power to its different quarters. It is a utopian vision, and the relationship of my work to his is inevitably complex; given that the situationists rejected art forms such as poetry in favour of the revolutionary transformation of everyday life, it's not strictly possible to write situationist poems. I am nevertheless fascinated by relationships between the poem, the embodied self and its environment, whether urban or rural; I'm sceptical of utopias, yet want the poem to become a space in which one might catch glimpses, however passing or fragmentary, of other possibilities. These exist in the past and future, hence always in motion. Creating forms that allow different kinds of movement becomes a way of opening space to time, and therefore change: although my poems have something in common with maps, they are often concerned with ground-level negotiations that shake up the static lines of a map's view. Like language, architecture makes categories: inside or outside, we or they—and the city as a concept depends on a bird's eye perspective that unifies it as a whole in opposition to its outside. Of course such distinctions are provisional, and I'm drawn to both the shaky illusion of what holds us, whoever 'we' might be, together, and the desire to open this to the foreignness that lies on the other side of walls or skin.

The Museum for Disappearing Sounds

exhibit 1

in breath a crackle of static
disturbance
        a detuned radio in one lung

drones erase each other
        electricity sings in D
tyres slur across the street

a shoreline just out of sight
        at the base of the skull

you hold the rise
and decay in its arc
        before dispersal
in wind on the microphone

cough in wave forms
count the layers

but when the light goes quiet
you sleep under air
              roaring
through the tunnel of your throat

exhibit 2

today I'm dripping into forests
        far into sleep
where you can't find me
cannot catalogue the rustle of larch
unpick
      pixel by pixel
the stones under my feet

exhibit 3

in thin vibrations of the phone
a voice shimmers on the end of a line

while outside
                    ring dove calls
slip over branches into memory

breath hops and starts
                    is this is this is this is this is this
I vanish in lossy compression

birds listen
                    come in and drop out

the rhythms that cradle us
turn to an I–you stammer of ringtones
on the nervous system's high whine

exhibit 4

in a frame of silence
                                the spectrum
                    shivers into transmission

in a forest of black and white
off-channel   branches
interlace over water   dark
            and interrupted light

the moon is close   closer
or retreating
behind the traffic far off

                    coming and going
accelerates to slow-mo as rhythm
turns to pitch and sinks to drone

110 / Zoë Skoulding

The Old Walls

The wall is who we are and they are not and
      farther in the boundaries collapse in a rush of
      security as cells multiply and break through stone
translucent grit cracks the skin open to the elements
      we go down through layers and this is history
      a low door at the foot of the walls opens into starry
arches articulate as loin bones the slender joints
      lithe as a voice disappearing from behind the
      words behind the walls where water moves
against deep tones of trees that cloud the air
      behind the smell of wet earth the voice leaves
      the shape of itself and the footprints of walkers
trace the shell of the city its dead words
      we crawled out of our words tender like snails
      and the new city grows from the loins of the old
as lichen spreads in acid maps invading and
      retreating the city runs along fingers runs along
      roads and wires and into fields and the sightlines
run back to the city in wires and the walls
      keep nothing out and the nothing beyond as a cloud
      of eyes moves through the streets and falls like rain

The Baths of Amnesia

Cool sulphur soaks the poison
                              out of bones
          a body modified
                    by lead
                    wine
the poisoning of time
                    that makes it money
          the coins of time   sunk
                              in copper verdigris
a ripple of light
              refracted on the ceiling
          voices float
                         am I at sea here
                    I swim
away from myself
                         talk politics or cellulite
just off the ring road
              an inner space slathered in nut oil
                         for leisure read hypochondria
                         retreat
          to the turquoise edge
              of tonic and loss
                         I could dissolve
                              the ear submerged
we held our noses to drink the stuff
                              blood pulsing in the head
                    the crackle of
          the nervous system   bones
                                   in heavy water

Castle

all defences rise in a few straight lines
         all sprung with traps
a curtain tower edging into weather
         foundations in rock
the walls run with drops of green
         as the sides of a glass
resist the flanking fire the enemy
         deflected in mirrors arrow slits
loopholes of light the glint of an eye
         sweat on skin trust me
as winter comes through walls of
         these foreign stones another
country coming through the cracks
         the ramparts wind around
the wind passing on her breath is
         safety durability and strength
will laugh a siege to scorn
         the oak door booms an entrance
above the shopping mall above the stability
         of violence trust me forever

❖

Zoë Skoulding (born 1967, Bradford) has lived in north Wales since 1991. She currently works at Bangor University where she holds an AHRC Fellowship and co-ordinates part-time literature and writing courses. She became editor of *Poetry Wales* in 2008 and is a co-editor of *Skald*, which she launched in 1994. She is a member of the group Parking Non-Stop, whose album *Species Corridor* was released in 2008 (Klangbad). Her collections are *Tide Table* (Caernarfon: Gwasg Pantycelyn, 1998), *The Mirror Trade* (Bridgend: Seren Books, 2004), *Dark Wires*, with Ian Davidson (Sheffield: West House Books, 2007) and, most recently, *Remains of a Future City* (Seren Books, 2008).

HARRIET TARLO

When I began writing in earnest, around 1990, I wrote only outside. I began with very short lyrics, edited almost to vanishing point, and moved on to sequence poems, written over a lengthy period of visiting and re-visiting a particular place. This "radical landscape" work was and, arguably, still is at the heart of my poetic practice and indeed my poetics. Early on, I became drawn to the complexities of the relationship between poet and place, word and thing, and excited by the open form techniques which I inherited via Richard Caddel who in turn drew on the American tradition inherited via Basil Bunting. Ric and I shared a particular love of Lorine Niedecker's work. Later, sound became increasingly central, and hearing (and writing about) poets such as Maggie O'Sullivan and Geraldine Monk helped tune my ear. Throughout this early period, I was also studying feminist and gender theory and this played an important part in my academic life, in particular my PhD on the poet H.D. It also led to connections with women who were influential on my work, especially Julia Ball, the artist, and Wendy Mulford and Frances Presley, poets whose work is also represented here.

When I think about gender in my work, I remember an essay I wrote about shifters which seems significant now—I have always played around with pronouns in poetry. 'A Spoon for Stein' is another form of play, the only poem I have ever salvaged from joining in creative-writing workshops I am leading. It is also of course a tribute to Stein via her *Tender Buttons*, a text talked back to in a far more sustained way by the American poet, Harryette Mullen, just one of many American poets from Stein to H.D., Fraser to DuPlessis, who have inspired me. Recently I have found women's lives surfacing in my work in a way that I did not particularly expect, influenced of course by the birth of my children, a renewed association with the domestic and with the wider circle of women. The work presented here consists of some of these short lyric pieces and selections from a longer work which represents an even newer departure. In 'Country House', I work for the first time with interior spaces, specific and generalised and am more interested in historical perspectives than in previous work. At present, I am working on and in local fields.

A Spoon for Stein

a curve is a centre if you turn it a round over which
you don't let in substance or do using it using
it in a baby mess throw a curve out of which came
came substance steal a spoon steel it filling
filling the curve is an ending end the handle and
mush the baby out of a stainless mess a stain
is not an object out of a spoon it curves round
around its filling is a centre throw it a spoon
is a missile hit and miss a spoon a mush onto and
of banana rice pear chicken potato apple
again spoon spoony tune let it go throw

[untitled]

we can see the animal
distorted by refinement
protruded extruded lips
eyes outlined costs involv-
ing imitations of another
animal's fur hair dyed ash
grey glassed eyes reflect
back a pair the same dis-
guise when we stood
upright

[untitled]

hands on feet, feet on hands
we balance/ she pushes forward
into the future with her legs/
my feet land/ trying not to smash
into the patterned glass door/
ornaments/ the nest of tables
stood below our mother's
mother's portraits ranged
serene, serene, serener even,
a smooth face/ in her thirties/
where we landed

Plaster Relief

wooden shutters in narrow boards floor

unevening grand mirrors to catch candle

light warm stuff in window dust

biscuits mildew nicks tapestry

hanging eagle fireplace coal

slag neo-classical plaster

work — motif motif motif — grapes

dangle, leaf patterns, Greek

vases doilies below stucco

above variations on a

theme winning over

the nobility

from 'English House'

Camellia House

       hazy blooms through
          outside
North stone face   South glass face
         circuit
       mildew-misty panes

        door creaks in

                a certain temperature
iron brackets elevate
         almost unscented
glass   space   paths through
          and under
     humidity

         contains
         green shine
         pink white sweetmeats

                 soft falling
            thuds
        a rest?   a decay?

flower towers
for the lady, her exotics   never shatter their shrine

     grafting and pruning   *all we do*
now is feed 'em

keeping it all down to scale

       underneath, roots wide-creep

Inside Story

High under hills and low over surfaces

      following through the last dance

      trying to surf it   sweet sanctimony

        of the few remaining

dancing through the furniture

   all that old wood

   not to fossilise   Arabesque! Arabesque!

      over the bookshelves, desks, locking cabinets

their pretty previous selves

     before the war   after the war

       weight-bearing each other

pose, pose again   on the sprung wood floor

    suddenly see him, seated,

    quizzical, two years gone

    spying through the sweet

    curled arch of her back   her torso

 flips over alive, alive

in all the sideboards, wing chairs, occasional

    tables, flourish and curlicue get out, ectoplasmic

      out of the ballroom, the studios   push against

     the inside air

       for always

Away

        adrenalin heat   it

slipped into

her bag   under his cape

                        riding

       her away

       passing it

            on

eat it now, eat it today

            warm laugh   a sliver

                  of wedding cake

blood–hot flush

keep it quiet

           put it on display

      brazening face

                a quick slaughter

         make it to

      another day

❖

Harriet Tarlo is a poet and academic whose books include *Love/Land* (Cambridge: rem press, 2003), *Poems 1990–2003* (Exeter: Shearsman Books, 2004) and *Nab* (Buckfastleigh: etruscan books, 2005), as well as publications in anthologies, journals and magazines. She also writes academic essays on modernist and contemporary poetry with particular attention to "radical landscape poetry" and gender. She recently edited a *How2* special feature on eco-poetics and is currently editing a new collection of radical landscape poetry for Shearsman, titled *The Ground Aslant*. She works part-time as a Senior Lecturer in Creative Writing at Sheffield Hallam University and as a freelance writer on creative projects and workshops.

CARRIE ETTER

By the mid-nineties I had been writing and publishing poetry for over ten years; this work consisted primarily of autobiographical personal narrative, a mode which felt like a tightening yoke. I began to despise literal accounts of episodes from my own life as a default approach to poetry and looked less to schools than individuals who pursued interesting alternatives, including John Ashbery, the Ted Hughes of *Crow*, Medbh McGuckian, Susan Wheeler, and Cole Swensen, among many others.

This reading led me to the exploration of a poetics of consciousness, which continues to this day. In such a poetics, the traditional concept of a poem's meaning tends to be beside the point, with any understanding gained experientially rather than through the comprehension of a linear argument. In other words, reading's goal is not to decode but to inhabit the text on its own terms. I think people could enjoy a much wider range of poetry if they stopped asking, "But what does it mean?", and instead went with the experience the poem offered, in the way many approach abstract art.

In 'Paternal,' for example, I investigate the depth and breadth of the upset of my father's critical illness by equating a parent with a foundation stone, then exploring its literal and figurative erosion. The poem courses among ideas of architecture, geology, meteorology, popular culture, etc. in a way that mimics a heightened consciousness roving from one subject to another to another and back again. The other poems here, like most of my work in a poetics of consciousness, are not interested in personal experience but in ideas, explored through an interaction of abstract thought and concrete world.

Divining for Starters (71)

in the quick of my wine

and trampling of sentiment

crucible of unrequited

walk down and down

nothing left to say

or there's no appeasing

tentative on the ice

beauty I'd have beauty

quick into dearth

the steep pitch

proclivity predilection intention

make of it *mi fabbro*

Prairie

sprawling through night   a train's low horn
the crossings   empty   the ritual
maintained   reflex or   especial precaution

do the sleepers hear it   do their ears
make unconscious record   to litanize

prescience loses particularity   unbound
on prairie   to vague expectation
with or without   hope

with or without   the train whistle's
thread   reminder redeemer

of silence   each isolate mind
banked in prescience   if it's not nostalgia
impalpable   in small hours   impalpable

in the drift   as names ease from objects
unmannered ritual   especial   withoutness

A Starkness in Late Afternoon

afternoon light   on stone   is immediacy
thought or   in itself
immaculate unsundering

the geese's flight   their warm
indivisible bodies   as much as   on the path
coarse stone   a single feather

and here I go   tearing the quilt
apart   patch by patch   all parts
no one   no one will love

on the storm–   fed sea   the wrath
the men and I   all prey to
praying to   the sea god

the high waves could be   suppose it
myrmidons   unnamed abettors
our fear   unchanged unchanneled

our prayers   scattered invisible

Paternal

A parent a plinth. The first week he regarded hospital as hotel. So the variables include the kind of stone, its consistency, the velocity of prevailing winds. What's purer than an infidel's prayer? How strangely, in the second week, the swollen limbs stiffened. And the effects of climate change: milder winters, more precipitation, two, three heat waves each summer. All American, non-Jewish whites are Christian by default. Incredulous, I realise his bicycle may rust and walk it to the shed. Such an ordinary act of reverence. The pulmonologist, the neurologist, the family physician. A bed is a bed is the smallest of bedsores. Blood doesn't come into it. Ritual, of course, is another matter. A Midwestern town of that size exhibits limited types of architecture. I've yet to mention the distance. Come now, to the pivot, the abscess, another end of innocence. In every shop, the woman at the till sings, "Merry Christmas," a red turtleneck under her green jumper. I thought *jumper* rather than *sweater*, a basic equation of space and time. Midnight shuffles the cards. Translated thus, the matter became surgical, a place on the spine. Each night the bicycle breaks out to complete its usual course. A loyalty of ritual or habit. "ICU" means I see you connected to life by wire and tube. A geologist can explain the complexities of erosion. The third week comes with liner notes already becoming apocryphal. Look at this old map, where my fingers once stretched across the sea.

❖

Carrie Etter grew up in Normal, Illinois and lived in southern California from age 19 to 32. There, she edited *Out Loud: The Monthly of Los Angeles Area Poetry Events* and coordinated several poetry reading series. In 2001, she moved to England, where she is Senior Lecturer in Creative Writing at Bath Spa University. Her first collection, *The Tethers*, was published by Seren Books in 2009, and her second, *Divining for Starters*, will be published by Shearsman Books in early 2011; pamphlets include *Subterfuge for the Unrequitable* (Elmwood, CT: Potes & Poets, 1998), *Yet* (Nottingham: Leafe Press, 2008), and *The Son* (Old Hunstanton: Oystercatcher Press, 2009). Her poems have been widely published in such journals as *Angel Exhaust, Arshile, Aufgabe, The Iowa Review, Jacket, The New Republic, Oasis,* and *The Times Literary Supplement*.

LUCY SHEERMAN

My work is concerned with mediating and remembering experience. The desire to achieve a mutual and shared sense of history is countered by the proprietorial urge of the individual to possess, manipulate and take control of narrative. The impulse to write and read memoirs, to steal and dissemble, fills my reading and writing with personal imaginative projections and false memories. My reading habits are eclectic and restless but Susan Howe and Lyn Hejinian are long-standing points of reference, along with the writers that I published in rem press.

Early memories and experiences are a recurrent theme in my work, particularly focusing on recollections by my maternal grandmother. My writing attempts to locate a fixed point of belonging, an effort which is elusive, transitory and naïve. Often the work integrates remembered experiences and reconstructs them as a collective, interrelating narrative. It is a process that introduces conflict between different, sometimes warring, states: ideology, consciousness, family, ownership and interpretation.

Work with a strong visual quality appeals to me—I'm interested both in the fetish of the word, with all its aesthetic and sensual properties, and in the role of language in the presentation of a visual register. Louise Bourgeois and Sophie Calle are among the artists whose work resonates. This visual sensibility bleeds into my writing practice; my work has been produced in limited editions, as pieces incorporated into installations and one-off commissions written for specific readings and events.

The poems selected for this anthology are from the sequence 'cher shed', which attempts a partial reconstruction of the past by accumulating and assembling fragments of recollected memory, speech, found text and objects. Various narratives are set down, interrupted and distressed. Flashes of reconstructed memory are destabilised by their dislocation from authorial voice or context. Some fragments are damaged beyond repair, the loss of meaning final and irrevocable. Fear of such loss is expressed as difficulty and resistance to a too final reading in the text. However there is also pleasure in the seepage and clumsy stitching of the poems which are full of cuts, gashes and scars as well as a gothic appetite for the drama of loss they play out. The title is a piece of found text taken from a gravestone where the letter 'I' had disappeared.

Somewhere My Love

hush while shimmering
she drifts backwards
against tide turning

inside cover let
names left listed
meaning to write

upon a once
only hesitant lost
first last breath

pent into skin
omits to mention
sinking without trace

forgetting the time
she stops to
watch season reverse

left foot into
right foot bootless
stamps shadow boxed

in negative prints
sole into sand
sunk sucked smooth

my life is
inside out my
lapses left longer

now the words
fall onto path
leaves there lies

my sister tears
off shoes stepping
into water blankets

stripped cold binding
sea lapped edges
this peninsula existence

Mine

The heart honeycombed; its collected spread
of prospects accrued in court precincts. Late
afternoon. Windows blazing. Walls gilded.
Sudden Suburban stillness. Sunbury.

Gold seams thread the fabric of the in thing
necklace boxed unthreading thirty years from
hand to throat spun into strands. Locketed.
The ache worn threadbare. Later years alter.

Settling. Sedimentary. Paint coats
over paint work. The lustre lost. Wake a
while. Blanket folds under fingers unfurled.
Feathers, leaves, stones, square the edges. Weighted

Down. Memories sink sleep deeper unmazed.
A king's picture — as I had dreamt of him —
chest covered in blood; heart on the outside.
Don't worry. Sound carries meaning intact.

Kutna Hora

(i)
light slants slivered
splashing around ankles
absorbed stops rain
bright sporadic plains
smooth over puddles
silence silver edged

unjust oppression sways
worst possible weather
knotting brow spent
skimming the senses
intimating skin feeling
out supposed extent

stalking through water
adjacent places unsettled
composure slipped up
exposing spring mechanism
deft hand touches
light speaking implied

piled stones imploring
look flew latched
onto likely subsidence
clings to surface
while water slips
convinced into ground

desperate climb down
infraction of place
breaks into angels
crashing down dust
particles subside light
picked gilt rays

spelt without accent
opaque intent spoke
volumes deflated either
mist or smoke
buttresses flying light
guttered into drains

(ii)
tongue into toxic
drops dry ink
into margins I
suppose all my
notes are ruined
page absorbing sky

pivoting earth pores
over faces sip
tiles set slight
shine gulped again
fades into dustless
blood caressing skein

spun delicately clung
fresh left trace
footprints sulked out
water spun stories
rush of water
darkness breathes still

door slammed into
secrecy surrounds place
its composed rapture
architecture addressed to
heavens in closure
shelled inside space

echoes cryptic inscription
skeleton key cut
unknot mortal coils
figure outing louder
many hands make
wholly earth upheaval

impulse buy repulsion
nave to chapel
planets aligned accordingly
invisible influence clouded
judgement spent snapping
movement stillness arbitration

(iii)
forced aspirants whisper
emphatic clatter besides
which was wetter
whether clarity seeps
sliding 600 metres
out of mind

day lid shut
striving blind in
sub strata lips
under mine sliding
every which way
sifting inscrutable pleasure

mapping out memory
step across space
feet worn smooth
metal foundered currency
skin clings porous
eyes shining smothered

ear shot spinning
curse hinged thought
over arm swing
spends forces striking
clinks into account
fresh phrase coined

crowns cold crushing
drinks songs drenched
surge over noise
gloves stoved hand
round hot drink
stealing lyric contempt

almost lost delivery
train into night
rain tempered glass
breaking in the wake
last delved fragments
read them through

she calls at the wheel oil

1 a.m. crossing fields

> reality outran apprehension
> her gaze floating
> across the space

moon shadows he cast

> slip-shod grip
> glamour satinised tip
> toes she teetered

stone still as she steps

> over weighted either
> down or up
> wrought thought out

through glass like paper

> tongues erased taste
> buds into palette
> spread to edges

fingers tear frail marks

> threading words on
> to throat caught
> on needle stuck

in white sheets shining

> steel into flesh
> steals the breath
> held last grasp

a minute rolled back

                                succinctly spoken so
                                lips spelt outer
                                pained or art fully

strains to sense of weight

                                light creased up
                                the bare word
                                kiss breaking silence

telling no one outside

❖

Lucy Sheerman was born in Wales and grew up in West Yorkshire. She set up the rem press poetry series with Karlien van den Beukel and ran the Poetic Practice Seminar with Dell Olsen and Andrea Brady. She is currently a literature specialist at the Arts Council, working to support the development of writers and new writing.

She completed a PhD in Literature at the University of Cambridge, her thesis examining the relationship between language writing and space. Her own critical and creative writing, focusing on experimental poetic practice, has been featured in a variety of journals and online magazines. She lives with her partner and two children in Cambridge.

REDELL OLSEN

The sequence 'A Newe Booke of Copies', from which this anthology's extracts have been chosen, exists on the page and as a live performance with video. Whether as text or as performance, this sequence offers frames and statements that can only be glimpsed in extracts and in ways that make any accompanying statement of its poetics necessarily partial. This said, it is also true that 'A Newe Booke of Copies' writes through a number of sources and materials relating to penmanship, needlework and their conflicting histories. The interest of such sources and materials is not merely historical, but suggests a clothing for the concerns of a 21st century poetics. One obliquely relevant source is an Elizabethan Writing Book also entitled *A Newe Booke of Copies*, first published in 1574. This book highlights rules and directions for correct handwriting in a variety of hands or styles. The first book of its kind to be printed in movable type, it marks a shift in power from the biblio-calligrapher to the printer. Medieval scribes, like embroiders, are mostly lost to anonymity. They usually did not sign their work. The individuality of the writer or seamstress is caught or glimpsed in the flourish of the decorative pattern, in the margin or on the collar of a garment. By contrast, perhaps the earliest dated British sampler to have survived was by Jane Bostocke in 1598. Her sampler is from a period of transition in the practical use of embroidery. Contemporary with such shifts, the ruff is taken by many people to epitomize Elizabethan high fashion. Ruffs were often covered in embroidery and seemed to have enacted an extremity of ornamentation which marked the status of the wearer. Given shortages of paper, damaged clothes were recycled into the rags used to make pulp for paper. This new copy of 'A Newe Booke of Copies', from which the extracts are taken, creates conflictual and conceptual flicker across these varied contexts already authored by diverse hands. Unattributed illuminations and rough copies in whitework are re-sampled. This new copy proposes a recutting of quills into new habits and a readdress to any "neat historical shirt". The emergent texture proposes a needlepoint to question and complicate its fastenings, rearranging its partlets for events as yet unknown.

from A Newe Booke of Copies

the ruff is the least parte of
itself surface stitchery never
merely flowers flaunt I is
assured curve strong to coil
of flickes and velvets calling
carnations pansies oak leaves
water monotone black silk
on white linen thin cambric
lighter lawn of stuff wrought in
black silk I of *Anatomie of Abuses*
geometric pattern outlines
easily copied in stem
chain back and double-running
from bookprint ruffle wearing
made out of England forbidden
to those under the degree
of baron and to women
below a knight's wife wrought
open worked down own middle
geegawes an other alphabet
of awful size worn starching
trimming-houses set up for
these devils cartwheels to use

a man wishes musical must know
tunes or how contingencies chose

in good steel or sharp towards no
proper control avoids too hollow

bodies cut off an inch above part
plant in wing remove feather I

I say marrow the cut should be
made away from the groove fork

formed thumb index then pare
down to beak of ploughshare

or sparrow symmetrical cut on
inner angle to point tiny piece

angles not on right bevels flow
freely divisible two more than

properly tempered whetted keen
thimble against colour to skin

correct manner shoulder points
taken from the right wing day

istrian galls soaked in wine
sieved through thickest linens

charged ink-horn blacker letters
ragged and faint for wishing

lays down rules graven errors
held with first and second rest

third middle fingers brake tilt
full body or edge alone cut

according to size letters against
backgrounds of coloured paper

bec at the nib and mouth calls
compels to bark not proper yet

protofeathers presence quill

knobs on posterior forearm

secondary feathers anchored

to bone follicular by ligaments

feathered dinosaurs made for

writing as currerbellellisacton

sandeliot or
gorge larson colours thread

Jane Bostocke metal
thread pearls beads
silk on linen back
chain ladder button
hole detached cross
arrowhead interlacing
pattern couching coral
cross-stitches speckling
bullion and French knots

ALICE LEE WAS BORNE

the lover has been greatly
simplified and the lady has
assumed vegetable form

mark move toward
looped-up chains
place calles partlet
stand collar to caul

a bunch of cherries
latticework white
with a bone sleeve
face ribbone across

stayned black beset
bodys upperbodies
encrusted chinnes
ornamental line or

pearls tied draped
bows husband smock
project wings setting
buskpoints unknown

slits aglet to decorate
puffed sects spangells
underlayed pad casing
feet fold mask of hem

inserts bell before
falling vertical lawn
ship sooner rigged
as arrowing trained

whalebone inserts
hanging in attention
circumferance doubt
casings tied of gold

in symmetry two
stiffen paddings
white with hooks
to disappear body

whole waist wired
rushes parts stays
sleeves of smock
slashes to show

adorn puff detach
small pinnes comfit
many cuts laced or
strings cut placing

usually starched us
as the underlying
marigold or daisy
this visible studded

pleats to the head
her ear the pinned
jewels quatrefoils
forepart detachable

partlets set pattern
matching as made
not a closed one
slits frill in attach

unmarried blackwork
patterned vine low
turned back impair
proportions huge

pleat so choicely
tied so desire hath
I might rest mine
arms on it suckling

difficult to say many
hours at starch and
pleat an unknown
farthingale tabbed

self border busks
and stiffening say
hath not some ruff
elegance knotted

this blood stained
cuff details shapes
cut work gossamer
fine white drawn

shirt survivor smock
damage at pinning
gape neck gusset
bows now missing

two insertions wide
linen stay tape face
strain on the point
of dear held display

❖

Redell Olsen is a poet and visual writer whose work includes performance, writing and installed texts. Her publications include *Book of the Fur* (Cambridge: rem press, 2000), *Secure Portable Space* (London: Reality Street Editions, 2004) and, in collaboration with Susan Johanknecht, *Here Are My Instructions* (London: Gefn Press, 2004). She is the editor of the online journal of *HOW2* (How2journal.com) which publishes modernist and contemporary innovative poetry by women, as well critical writing about such work. She is a senior lecturer at Royal Holloway, University of London and the course director for the MA in Poetic Practice.

ANDREA BRADY

The first poem I wrote, in 1982, was prayerful heroic couplets about the Lebanese hostage crisis. As a teenager the poems I most loved were oracles of transport; writing was a means of testifying charismatically to the perfectability of things. It was a tribute to the unachieved, its billowing references blowing around the outside of the feeling that was all beginning. Poetic language, like love, has always been a kind of bounty, correlating to something that wells up and is no speech: an infinity of opportunities to be exact.

And that was the risk; all those opportunities might be spent at the fuzzy edges of exactitude. I might forget to mention the apparatus, the movements and characters of most days. Though I work the facts hard my radicalism does not feel very modern to me. I wish I could be funnier. I admire my contemporaries who polish off the superfluity of things, who inventory all the commercial vehicles for the average life; but the economy of my poetry can't manage that, even if it lives off the same flow of cheap credit. Where I make use of the personal it is as a dialect of the present. My poems plot the contour lines of international argument as ripples and distortions of the local. And they have a weakness for ornament, which I try to keep in check. Though I have always lived in cities I grow tight without the beautiful air.

But the anger, what is its relation to this bounty? As the impulse to begin in poems, to make an image of the perfectability which comes on like a trance, weakens, I shunt my desire for freedom into poems: and mourn there, and organise there, the lost worlds. But what comes first for any of us? Is critique grafted onto something more rootless, a turn in character? For a long time I wished that the world were better, as good as art. Now I am learning to write about happiness.

My infant daughter has begun to sing. Her body is flooded with the desire to participate in the comedy of communication: from her curled tongue to her bucking feet she is electrified with the joy of sounding. Her better capacity reveals the really possible infinity of speech itself, which renews itself at any time, without effort or commiseration.

The Real and Ideal

Do not divorce your body from the field.

The darger draws the asphalt track up
and out of the uncut grass, away to the left.
There with an unbleached head
goes the younger girl, a peer for turning in place
drive the lightening of endless choices through her sock:
free price, free will, jogging out towards a remote end
in a secret city. All ends are remote, and not least

this day, dispersed over the map by its content.
Flowing with energies drawn off voices
cycled from speech given in gift and with
perfected sense of understanding.

It seems like nothing. When you missed your calling
you were probably wrapped
in butcher's paper, warm, mixed, fatty.
So many times you have found it there

It looks outside the footprint of this house
like a magic workshop, tumbling in mechanics
and flash memory, toppling
on the verge of a language which hardly knows
it needs it. From this mist is safe deposit
as if the bulk were still erasable,
or the scholars born by exponent
would in future fail to discriminate our values.
Everyman was a pervert, they'll say,
his dog microchipped and neutered, and the users
generally agreed in theory.

But don't don't suck the air out of a bladder
and let it turn your head: beyond sea foam
or the fortunate in Star City

such empty spaces best uncontemplated.
Content kills the war of fact, people
in zoos and the million subtle relations
which emerged only into prose in the age of things.

That kid over there lacks content, and so moves.
Happiness is the end of all politics,
where the day worker comes to rest behind a film.

The film moves. It shows wings,
wings beating slow as resting hearts
magic lanterns balanced on parades of grass—
or maybe they are just hearts.
And they move. They are braced for the end.

Still Hanging on Clinton's Second Visit

Hope for running out on the flats, under
the overpass that chutes this abstract
into bread home delivery, buckled up
from your front porch to my front seat.

The hyphenated bridge lane where motor
boards a dream of expansive happiness,
dinosaurs trapped in oil pits, a future
to run into red and green eyes

and out till no man's land. Past the refinery
into outlaw verde, unowned hydrotropic
life unclinched by regularity, ownership,
by a loss that has never happened: one of the

kinds of possible losses. You sang this
national anthem, your life parenthesized
by flight into cinema and depiction:
the sun sets orangely, tempers cool

the boss goes nowhere and the land,
lived from, bossily patriotic. Your name
retrieved from the web, the collocation
with the smash given to know

the unknown, blood furls gradually
from the heads and is never less
parenthetical. Texts still bundled
in your pocket switch to discreet mode, rings

engage the natural world in decoration.
Above the concrete marshes, the stars
can't make their empty lines believable.
Stars to shadow by, chase out of manhattan

where that marsh is brown and the old worlds
creep around on stilts with eeling baskets.
Banality will never be obsolete, like the internal
combustion engine: even the tracks

of unbroken yellow too fleet for
the escape artist, a mimic pile-up loops
in place of persons, in a question of sovereignty.
No place unmandated, no stretch without

the service stations marked in bold on the route planner.
These four lanes a horn of plenty blow out at night
the endless hunting lament, a fictional
surplus for continents learning to recognise their bounds.

In the outlaw west the wedding party tips
their guns into starlight glasses, fill space
with pellets to celebrate the belly's axle; fire
falling down burns a noose free, ash and sand

to put fires out and secure a slipless exit. Was this
really what you wanted, to splurge on a rider

the whole real an advert break? Do go on so,
then breath undeterred in the breakbeat meter,

singing for freedom to misuse national space:
the free ride which is no freedom
when at the edge of disaster
you find yourself in the back seat of the patrol car,

the reel catapults into pitch black, and over all of us
who still live the stars
crash down from their heroic outlines
into vacancy

Cultural Affairs in Boston

She Cannot Take Any Credit For This One.

Slingshot from the rust belt
comped to the commonwealth,
keep your eye out for the mass spikes
puritan sign: the horizon gets uppity, folk
       picking on their porches in the dashboard
       picking sacred harps in cartoon cloudland—
we're getting religion as endless corduroy
bends upward into blue hills. What kind of relics
will we be,   toxic twinkies
        haughty french dressing
please end on a high note, and let our spoils
full pay with interest on the departmental i.o.u.

Pilgrims spill out of the suburban,
the regular army training in sculls
points us up the Charles towards Winthrop
and guacamole from Grendel's kitchen,

Robin tears his Reuben limb from limb.
   By the sword we seek peace, but peace
   only under liberty. 85¢
tokens for the T; that is the same 7-
eleven, same shoes, adulthood
    condensed by rackrents
keeping warm the original settlement
like a fur fringe to a sad perturbation.
   These hauls are ok
   you can get warmer, thanks
to Bouchard's booklist starting at the beacon,
make our way across the common.
If the ghost of Joy Street could tell
us where to locate
     cheap sex, oysters, beanfeasts,
Pusey and Lamont have nothing on him
or the boys who washed their clothes in buffalo.

Offload the surplus at barker is mounted
the double veritas shield our sideline,
a final diminishable triplet makes good
as they can under the eyes of John Harvard.
   We do to gog as we've done to roam,
   a staged reading as the pretribulational event
afterwards it's hoped for a kind of rapture:
     may the poets be hung on hooks
     as catchy as the cola-mark turned to Love,
and this is how you speak to me now,
are you some kind of invading army?
Speaking to Sam and Dan, Nancy and David,
Michael and Michael and Teddy Roosevelt
and Percy Lowell, to the engraved Emerson
Bulfinch and Agassiz, to all of you and Chronos
billeted in the corner, bred from chaos to Rambo-
   sinewed adulthood, his jersey
   over his face like a blinded goal-scorer;
and to the inflatable clock keeping modernity

in check. The storm of debris lashing
the single-glazing, we retire to grafton
        to deflate the speech-balloon,
            kill the lights and unclip the roving
                        mike from disney wings.

Now bring forth the beast that ruled the world with's beck,
And tear his flesh and set your feet on's neck;
And make his filthy den so desolate,
To th' 'stonishment of all that knew his state.
Youtube ornithocaerus crumbles
by a water-source after his dumb mating dance,
took thermals to cross the ocean and set up
shack here with his condemned flock. So
I'm told by the little genius. Pups scramble around
bouncing Hazel, and the migrating
are their descendents or everybody's.
Making way for legal seafood, damp taleggio
and this Dialogue between England Old and New.
                        Joy street intaglio,
            faust ink hot on an infinite switch
hidden in potential until screwed to the paper.

Fine-Line Ghazal

Road noise waits at a skylight. Through breaks in
perpetual rain, light picks up your outline.

Business is done. The night wanders us in
to health, so the following meanings are fine.

As the true fiction in that frame is:
we assume a resting angle, not sick with wine

or drawing the thought out on trouble's bow
string, intrigued by the cut word, the broken line.

The globes can fire perpetually outward,
making the void free where they shine.

For nothing less than chance has spun them
into array, wrapped in oxides, a skinful in twine

wraps the self like a match. Who flares
and winds down alert in gold. No sign

of difference, except in the stems of the bond,
recognition prices each flutter of the spine.

This is an end of variety: to be sure,
that we are here, that your face is mine.

End of Days

> *in honour of Mohammed Haithem and Suleiman Mahmoud*

All radical signs by which on   These radical brackets all around
the component times, by which   We select   Good luck
beauty hard and shining like   Pearls, and   Lozenges
phrasing all these renegade times into the divine message. Choose
Choose to bless. Choose to bless the day falling
into brass jack pot. *I remember all
the days, they play before my eyes sometimes
I go to watch the ovens* rich in natural vitamins
feeding off myself, my dreamed-for.

For too long, sorting tickets in the shade of the thorn
that penny drops affixed to   Find
the opening palm these aces allude
to   this life, the desired, and even when dark
fills its haunches with ice and fire I have been on it,
on full voice coarse or passionated, a bundle of nerves

And each with their own head. As I go on I go
west idiotic, free to shout like nothing saffron.
I'll go to that country, the beautiful one

in the cockpit if I learn my trig. The sign says No
equivalence between those who take pride in dying
and those who vow   When speech is the real action
The sign is an impress blowing down and east out,
treadmills backwards to an origin where that time
split into component sprockets   Two incisors
splitting each other by their petty alignment. *If it's like this*
at the beginning what will it be like in the end The infant learns
to recognise his box by infinite difference   How
he discovers his father in the line up a testament
to his faith that he is made
for recurring   These times are familiar we
pluck our joys choosily from the sky before it
burns out the last branches.

❖

Andrea Brady was born in Philadelphia in 1974 and has lived in the UK since 1996. She is the director of the Archive of the Now (archiveofthenow. org) and co-publisher of Barque Press. Her publications include *Vacation of a Lifetime* (Cambridge: Salt Publishing, 2001), *Embrace* (Glasgow: Object Permanence, 2005), and the verse essay *Wildfire* (San Francisco: Krupskaya, 2010, originally published as a hypertext, dispatx.com, 2006). She has performed throughout the UK, Europe and US. Widely published in small magazines, Brady was one of four poets featured in a recent special issue of *Chicago Review* (53.1, 2007) devoted to British poetry. She teaches Renaissance and contemporary literature at Queen Mary University of London, and lives in London with her husband, Matt ffytche, and daughter Ayla.

Sascha Akhtar

In my work, writing poetry is distilling the essences of things: I equate the act with alchemy. I delve in translucencies; how the subrosa can be made potent with the position of a certain word next to another in a manner that may invert the dominant paradigm, as it were. It is the mystical that possesses me, and although my work appears to be very non-traditional it comes from a place of tradition; the Eastern poetic tradition.

In poetry of the subcontinent the word *haal* is commonly talked of when describing the "state" a poet has to enter in order to enscribe poetry. For me poetry comes from being in this *haal*, an otherworldly place. Poets like Faiz Ahmed Faiz are important, but equally Neruda and Guillame Apollinaire. The subject of love is a traditional one in poetry of the subcontinent and it is a place I write from, either ethereal or corporeal. I also appreciate the quotidian world; the Unreality as the Sufis call it. I write of loss, alienation, melancholy, remembrance and longing, and of a sense of being woman.

I believe our primary languages can narrow our sensibility, so I like to experiment with different modes of language, as it were. Sometimes this takes an extreme form as with *The Grimoire of Grimalkin*, sometimes mild, as in joining words to make one unit—something I learnt from Rumi.

Melancholy

with everything
there is an answer, writing
an answer

sketched on my nimbus
finger

there are two
dies cast

for each shoulder
rifling through your each ear
for germs of left last
dignity

many minds tampered
with and more

I was born in 1976.

★

this is about you
what have you seen
cold compress

two tracks simultaneous
an x

makes a point
to find

forget the bouganvillaea

breath learnt
who is speaking through speaking

melancholy, I-body.

I-Body 4

is there, there is
a past

only & present
quickly becomes
shuffle to

the next pan-destination

★

wipe footprints
off the floor

because I don't want to see them

everything has happened
before me

perhaps your voice
alone
is chopped
to cadence

if you end here, you.

★

are distorted

he will get up & want dinner
& tea

I will move effortlessly
in plural, in feminine

in subjunct

mellow life.

★

I-Body 5

I can't read
what I have somewhere

not written anywhere

but in this space of virtual
other

I can only find with click
shift

mind spewing.

The Sufi

Surrender I, speak

a word for you

a pot on flame melts
before we eat glistening
like cherrywinter, like bootblack
I polish indefinitely

reach my dizzy head
in all its circumference, touch
choose a card
save sure till you mean it
I'll clock your time in true beads
tonight I see a crash
next morning wizard hollers

a crest-fallen face, a dust-rudder

who was there on this winters morn
I saw snow-devils whirling
& lost myself.

wine pour backwards.

hold.

❖

Sascha Aurora Akhtar is an international writer with an anchor firmly in the UK. Her grandmother, born in Blackpool, was an English stage actress in 1950s London, who relocated to Pakistan for love. In 2004, half a century later, Akhtar came to settle in the UK. She attended the London Consortium but, unenamoured of academic life, left soon after. Finding the literary scene lacking in diversity, in 2006 she started up a reading series with Trinidad poet Anthony Joseph, *La Langoustine Est Morte*, which has been going ever since. Her debut poetry collection, *The Grimoire of Grimalkin,* was published by Salt Publishing, Cambridge, in November 2007. Her work has appeared in *Stimulus Respond, The London Magazine, Trespass, HOW2*, and *Skald*, and in 2008 she was named in *The Guardian* as one of the top ten to watch in the new poetry scene.

SOPHIE MAYER

In *Always Coming Home*, Ursula K. Le Guin offers a thoughtful summary of "Some Generative Metaphors," from "The War" to "The Way." A pivotal—and profoundly generative—metaphor for Le Guin is The Dance. She writes:

What it generates: Music
Universe as dance: Harmony. Creation/destruction.
Society as dance: Participation
Person as dancer: Cooperation
Medicine as art
Mind as dancing: Rhythm, measure
Language as connection
The relationship of human with other beings as dance: Horizontal linkings
Images of the dance: Steps, gestures, continuity, harmony, the spiral.

The Dance is where I discover my poetics: in movement and embodiment, in unfolding and foot-stamping, in connection and ecstasy. In strophes and verses, poetry is historically connected to the turns of the choral dance, yet how can we dance to contemporary poetic revolutions?

Turn again.

To turn images, bodies, histories into words—and vice versa, as cinema does, as choreography does. I can't resist flesh—on stage, on screen—and its compressed eloquence of desire and discovery. Into the wordless space of dance my verbal invention flows: words for that angle of the wrist, that flip, that stillness. And film is my lullaby, my dreamspace. Dancing filmmakers Sally Potter, Maya Deren and Abigail Child (all poets as well) returned the pivot of the foot to my voltas.

Turn again.

To turn language this way and that like a diamond catching the light, as Gertrude Stein did. To re-turn words to hidden meanings, as Cecilia Vicuña does. To turn stories inside-out, as Angela Carter did. It's an unashamedly feminist practice, this swerving from the main stream to explore different waters: deeper, darker, cooler, greener, haunted by women drowned and women diving into themselves.

Turn again.

To what returns, what rises up. Psychically, politically, or prosodically. What's *Resurgent*, to borrow the title of Lou Robinson and Camille Norton's anthology. Poetic returns on the model of the spiral (hinged on connection through intertext, conversation): diving inwards, reaching outwards. Towards.

Turn again.

As a planet. As a sounding of space, as an ecstatic trance, as a child's game.

Zero / navel

The first day in rehearsal, not the first hour but sometime
towards late afternoon, when everything was edging almost
gold, we stopped

and held each others' cocks. Bare as it sounds, it was: pants
down warming overworked ankles, navels half-exposed against
ragged T-shirt hems

whose limning insistently caught the eye. Mirror work, body exchanged
for body against that gap of abdomen; cotton lifting from the core—
pivots the drop. Fulcrum

and then: nothing. Not erotic but. Work. Dancing, we must touch
each inch of the other. With confidence – and in as well. It's
a weighing-up,

a grip no different than lifting Sylvie at the waist, or a shovel. Spade's
a spade, and we have things—memories, their movements—to dig
out of one another

like fragments from a bombed city. We have to balance findings
against what's lost. It's limbic. Circulating. Pulsing, even; turned
out but not on, except

as lights are. Aware: body as story. On my knees: scars; his back
knobbed with brittle bone. And these, between us, excavation
and its tools,

evidence and wound. Breath catch and in. Evaluation. Paler, thinner,
veined, warmer, silken. Shy. All movement focused in on navel, on
notmoving. Holding

still.

Import/Export

Late/x

Apparent is (apparently) enough. An extra p I feel beneath the mattress, all talk of readiness to take the plunge. But here in rubber sheeting, we have no ointment for that rash. How careless to become so irritated. Such a sap to crack at such viscosity. Imported what's important. Substitutes are military. Are susceptible. Are not available free at this surgery. Our wrecking ball comes first, all edginess and walls of flame. When lip slips. His squeak between. The gap that nothing whistled through. Will not regenerate. Pink water and the glitter inside whose descent unleashes. Punchline missed in the trawl for bone. Cracked and glazed. Illegal fish from coastal waters. It's getting late. Clock that: the rising seas will take their bow. Iridescent, the broken vow of care. Disrupted sleep. The flood of dreams. Potential clouds. Reform. And pour again, this time to pool. To crystallise in duct formations, neuronal synthesis. Of this: the sheet grows taut, a drumstruck skin. Resonance is distant, backward echo rising through the muffle. From whose perspective. The pea speaks. Her sleeping restless weight. And in the damp of morning, all is red disguised as white. Those patches there, they'll scar. Be seen, unsheathed and from the sky.

Theobroma

Foundation: bean from seed. Dark husk discarded for the meat. And sweetness, added all too soon, a cane for jaded palates. Continents as packaged goods: wrapped in gold and ribbon-tied, to give the lie when rot sets in. Abundance. None forged cleanly, powder and crumb littering the floor. And now they trade fair claims: scatter the sacred and consumed. How flattering. Presented as collection. No trifle. As always, dark liquid turned to gold and so to art.

Masonry of slab and bar. The halls to house the world with what's been taken. A moulded, fluted cake with surprise inside. And he who breaks his tooth, and she who chokes it down, shall be crowned the king and queen. Shall wear silver and purple crowns. Shall be foiled, stained with what melts. Blooms to white at their heated touch.

Cha

It is a ceremony of conjoinment and as one: black into white. Or otherwise. The swirl. The vows of steam. Fluctuant inhalation. Centrifuge with careful water and embrace. Burn to touch (through glass, clay, polymer or foam) and move away. Takeout. Must leak in order to become, must intervene but not dissolve. Dispersal as principle, molecular intermingling run up against borders (glass, clay, polymer or foam). So each different curvature will meet your hand, and each finger has its own behaviour. Though not cosmetic. Though it will dye. Stains the dry maps of once, preceding. Is all talk. Some say with salt and some with lemon. Some with rancid butter and some with wads of paper. Such healing for such great harm. Bricked as money. Picked under the sun and endlessly. Whiff of city port lands, ghost stream. Marsh flavour. Each cup containing its future, wet and fuming. To say nothing of its lumps. Such quiet silver to be so uncontained, a matted history (twist, uncover) remains when you are done.

FIRE / white warrior

And when I come
And when I come in
And when I come in white
And when I come in rising tides
And when I come in tides of white foam
And when I come in ripped shrouds and shreds
And when I come in trampling foam to dirty white
And when I cast from me these dirty filaments and fibres
And when I stand in the square and lift my lace so all can see
And when beneath my skirt you find my boots of steel
And when each petal has been eaten by barefoot girls
And when my finger wears no ring but of itself
And when I smear the ranks of you with sugar
And when I turn to flee on fire and wing
And when I leave this self and skin
And when I gasp down to bone
And when I am annealed
And when and when
the dress speaks

        back
            and beaded front
            and pearlèd arms
            and sequined bust
            and swagged skirt
            and boned waist

                        are gone

                  are armour & are gone

❖

Sophie Mayer is a London-based writer and educator. She writes about film for *Sight & Sound*, *Little White Lies*, *Vertigo* and *Chroma*, where she is a commissioning editor, and moderates the English PEN World Atlas. Her creative work has appeared in journals in the UK, US, Canada, the Republic of Ireland and Australia. In 2009, she published her first solo collection of poetry, *Her Various Scalpels* (Exeter: Shearsman Books), and two books about film, *The Cinema of Sally Potter: A Politics of Love* (Harrow: Wallflower Press) and, as co-editor with Corinn Columpar, *There She Goes: Feminist Filmmaking and Beyond* (Detroit: Wayne State University Press). She blogs (sporadically) about reading as *deliriumslibrarian*, and about feminism and culture for *Shebytches*.

Rachel Lehrman

Poetry—an awareness; a tool; an art; but most importantly a physical, cognitive and emotional experience. Words enter us. They change us. As poets we are especially vulnerable to their power; they are the instruments of our trade.

Poetry, however, is more than this. Along with words and their meanings—*music*. The shape of the mouth making the words. The subtle movement of the diaphragm. The pause between breaths marking out the rhythm of a piece. And in response to the meaning and movement of these words and silences—*recognition*—an emotional response in which some part of us beyond the intellectual and logical mind resonates with the cumulative experience: *poetry*.

When I write, I am guided by music and emotion, feelings and inspirations, images and rhythms just out of reach—by poetry itself. Words arrive, often on their own, and I rearrange, omit and change them in an effort to find and give voice to the poetry that I feel.

I have been described as a love poet; a female poet; a meditative, lyric and experimental poet. But where poetry exists, there are no labels—no designated forms. Trends and movements, writing techniques, narration and linguistic experimentation do not matter beyond their ability to contribute to the poetic experience.

That is, ultimately, what I seek—an experiential poetry. A poetry that appeals directly to the senses and elicits an emotional, psychological, spiritual and/or physical response in the reader. Language transcribes and contributes to this experience; it can, perhaps, evoke it. For me, however, the words are the score—the notes and rests that house the song; it is only in the playing that the true work comes to life and for that to happen the notes must be pure.

It is with this sentiment that I aim to move beyond 'the poem,' to the place where poetry exists without beginnings or ends or rules; past form and structure and into the true heart of the work—the essence of things.

from: **Nightscape**

I move with you as you step in the darkness. I follow as you bend to rub your legs with a towel.

You held me and you let me go . . .

Lying on your bed I hover a hand's length away. Feel outside of flesh where fingertips greet skin.

I cannot touch what isn't there.

I was there: the rush of wings, the soft tick in the walls that keeps you awake. See me in the mirror with you now.

Awake it sways overhead. My body stirs.

The body stirs opening our hand.

What it is to be awake outside of a body.

Orbit of throat and sleeve.   The difference— air.   The god piece slips.

I stop to listen where sleep begins.

Oh to be draped with skin, capillary, nerve—that four lips may press touched, touching.

Where it comes from night is an eyelid. Eyes reveal...

The whole reality in your head   projects from where we begin

where you   *. . . where I*   come from.

I will have
I will have

consciousness of heart and head,   the voice of a god
consciousness whole

aorta and skin—   the way to enter   /   *to enter*

~

Lying on my bed it hovers a hand's length away.
To define it is to put a hand on the groove above an eyebrow
to feel outside of flesh where fingertips greet skin.

press your nails against the wall

If I want in the right place
it's already with me
in my blanket hollowed like a lung.

Knees fill the backs of my knees.
Nipples press my shoulder blades.

your shoulder,   *where I rest my*   *hand*

The sensation of a voice: *sweet pea,*   *white january*
takes me from where my bones ache
from where I cup my hands against the wall and sing

when you sit-up nights, to look out your window
I rest my hand

when you   *press your head against the wall*
         cover your ears
         sit against the wall, counting till morning

~

Close to morning,
everything's black and moves
like a black crayon on a black mask.

There's an hour nothing speaks
except from behind the mask

[silence]

Breath lifts my skull, pushing
the full expanse of sky.
I feel what would be, if my head were sky
looking down at me.

[silence]

Walls break down. I become
myself for a moment, before they start back up.
The first rest on a long flight of stairs
reminds me what will be when I get there,

carries me, curls-up next to me in bed—
becoming my other, my other, lending me eyes
in place of arms, disguised as breath.

[silence]

~

We emerge. The skin on our lips flakes like dough.   Our tongues are
white. Small animal-like noises rise from our bellies.

~

I come back and find you
still rising, held
as a bird by weight of hand, hungry
like a bird strains its dagger beak
toward sun

something cries-out
from the depths
something cries out
I am
suddenly centered

breasts sway, small birthmark above the navel
dips

so many shapes
all   or none of them   beautiful

~

Was she my lover or my sister? I no longer remember. I can't. Leaves blur
a fury of light. Faces in a fury. A house or the house next to it? There's
nothing we can do unless we all fly out screaming, terrified, shuddering
in bliss. A white white world, like darkness, is indistinguishable.

Rachel Lehrman came to London in 2002 after completing her MFA in creative writing at the University of Arizona. Her work has previously appeared in *Blue Fifth Review*, *The Drunken Boat* and *Shearsman*. Lehrman has collaborated on a number of art projects in London including *Nomadics* (2005) and *Understorey* (2007). In 2004 a recording of her work accompanied an installation exhibited in the basement of the Hayward Gallery. That same year she exhibited her poetry in broadside format at the Camden People's Theatre. In early 2009, she completed a PhD in Collaborative Art at Roehampton University.

EMILY CRITCHLEY

My work has been described both as responding to the concerns and techniques of the American poets I studied for my PhD (Lyn Hejinian, Leslie Scalapino and Rosmarie Waldrop), as well as the context in which I did that study: Cambridge. The paradox here is key, for many of the poets and academics I met there, who importantly shaped my work, as well as my thinking about my work, were/are sceptical of Language poetics. The sense of conflict this gave rise to became somewhat of a living point of focus, both for my thesis, and for my writing. As Keith Tuma puts it:

> "mimicry of emphatic statement [often figures], as if the speaker were adopting the language of the poem's implied addressee in order to bring that language up short or to insert moments of silence and resistance within it, interrupting its rhetoric and its certainty." (*Chicago Review*, 53:1, p.215)

American daring, largesse even (from Pound to Berryman, Olson to Mayer) is something I've long since been drawn to in poetry; a rather more 'Cambridge' anxiety (to draw crude geographical analogies) over rigour or epistemological certainties is what I'm often struck by; grappling with the combination is what my poetry mostly does.

Added to this is the fact that my thesis concentrated on understanding socially the dominance of the Language scene by its male writers, while claiming feminism as one of their key political concerns, and here was the same pattern being repeated in Cambridge! Disappointment, as well as a kind of satirical defiance in the face of this situation, worked its way into much of my writing, including the poem reproduced here; at times the effect is supposed to trample even the poetry's thinking (as if over-intellectualizing were one of the key causes of hypocrisy). I wanted 'When I say I believe women' also to question the lines between poetry and academe (for instance, in the poem's power struggle between main text, side and footnotes), certainty and doubt, men and women, public façade and private behaviour. Such issues remain hugely important to me.

When I say I believe women...

When I say I believe women & men read &
write differently I mean that women & men
read & write pretty differently. Whether this is
biologically 'essential' or just straightforward like
when you left the toaster burning or
because women have a subordinated relationship
to power in their guts I don't know. Is this clear
enough for you to follow. I don't know. When I
say we should try not to forget the author, this is
because that would be
bad manners as well as ridiculous. When I say
there is a centre into which exclusion bends I
mean *nothing*. When I hear you ask how much
money did you get or how far have you got
into your work, something internal plunges for
the exit, like puking, it wants to get out—
because you're still being hostile (after all these
years)—& look toward the charcoaled
meats for rescue. There they are still on fire.

Sometimes seems to serve pretty obviously for exclusion & showoffs Or tumbleweed arranging So many times good women have written to me saying they can't subscribe not really out of shyness but rather "find i want to have something specific to *say and too often feel i don't have something spot-on to add right when it's needed" I wonder a lot of the men don't seem to have this inclination Might call it modesty or else losing heart

When I read your attempts at Latin & 'cum' & humour I think: no one cares about you after 1 a.m. &: it's so exhausting, &: did your father(s) never tell you to "stop showing off to people." Were you never crushed & leant on by another? I guess that's why my weariness comes from & distends. Or perhaps it's just obvious bad manners. When I get excited because I think, why should I hide the fact? Does that mean I have loose morals or absence (social awareness) or cool. I will pretend from now on. When I lose heart because there are too too many 'I's for my liking, & you won't write to me these days because you say I lost heart too many times, & that's ridiculous, but OK, because you're still hostile after all these years that are still there smouldering.

Wrote how terrified we were about the ongoing destruction of green spaces in England How it made you just want to 'get out'

Certainly where I grew up reading ~~Marvell~~ is being lost & overdeveloped & What would ~~C. Olson~~ make of such greenbelt catastrophe

Whenever I write *you* it blends & morphs into so many others. That's what comes from being informal I guess. Or not cool. Or erotic. When I get respite from absence, when I think about SPACE—annihilating all that's made . . . I don't know about presence (metaphysically), I never felt any. When that's all corrupt-ridiculous, a dream-trampling, I hear that Dundee's a satellite of Cambridge, I laugh & puke & think how nice to be a lesbian putting on plays by Olson. When I watch films with '70s headscarves on heroes like they were the good old days.[1] (But free love comes at a price, at least the cost of one or two burnt fingers). Our mothers learnt that for us amongst nothing.

[1] Shocked & surprised at the physical difference between say ~~Klute~~ ('71) & ~~Alex in Wonderland~~ ('70) Especially in that scene with his friend where they're talking about how his woman's a bad lay

Emily Critchley / 179

Always shocked &
surprised at how regularly
you put yourself 'forward' &
self-advertise Especially
when I think about Carla
Harryman, Kathleen Fraser,
Leslie Scalapino How they
try to avoid "fitting the
radical object into the
square peg of patriarchal
canon-making narratives"
~~"Women's Writing: Hybrid
Thoughts on Contingent
Hierarchies and Reception,"
1999~~

Because yes there were a lot
of things that were difficult
& not even that constructive
to follow (I find this about
academe generally)

The SPACE allowed around each satellite, you
want to crush it & plunge into an abyss of your
own name, obviously-shaped through the light,
even though self-naming is a fault & way too
semantic. Whenever you talk the people
salivate; others write "pretentious bullshit" in
the margins, underscored & overlined with
envy or malice or maybe just obvious good
sense. The pockets are full of stones. When
people hear you talk they think: you've got a
way with yourself—or: if it were me I'd run—
or: words. Or: way too erotic. When I say lips
like chances are the keys to all surface like a
true domestic animal, you should see into my
room, I haven't vacuumed in days. There is
almost no SPACE left.

Who just recently 'flipped
out' as Scalapino would say &
got committed There are so
many things he could
have said & done which has
taken a lot of time
~~to put into this bag of
nerves~~

~~I've been carrying around
with me ever since~~

What elements are in the vowel-sounds of your
mouth, too recent like carbon rings.[2] Anyone can
tell the interrogative is a style like any
other (apron). I'm wondering about nursing &
cooking & following you round, wiping the
saliva from your tongue. That body more
prompted like recent words dressed up in a
foul mouth that wonders about illuminating
gaps: no money, real work or outlets, just an
object which heeds, a verb without status.
Daughter's inconsequence unloosed on a
whole crowd of informals to no (obvious)
purpose.

[2] Rosmarie Waldrop: "When I say I believe that women have a
soul and that its substance contains two carbon rings the picture
in the foreground makes it difficult to find its application," *Lawn
of Excluded Middle*, 11

Didnt know what it had *meant* It was only then you got me thinking who'd had no long-term aim at all but ~~nonetheless found it hurtful you could just up & leave like that~~

In Paris this guy who'd watched me eat my floating island dessert alone He'd ~~said he liked women who looked lost & thought I could do with the company~~

That uninhibited experience told the time & your temperature without difficulty. There was no object to my supposing, but a verb with no status. When you told me to take it any way I wanted, I took it in the best sense possible. I guess that wasn't what you meant me to do. No object, no money, & no outlets. Woman's a floating island round an imperfectly-baked dessert. In an oven you get burnt. Is this too obvious are you getting warm or even angry. This isn't metaphorical, I mean it to be *true statements*, shook up like inside hurt. However you decide to take them. Do I look like I'm joking when I tell you that "The meaning of certainty is getting burned."[3]

[3] Rosmarie Waldrop, *Lawn of Excluded Middle*, 18

I once said you were the emery board to my fantasy, the CO_2 to my fire. In late adolescence you were pushed forward, they said your will was 'atypical.' I knew the main points. Implicit in all this was a fatal altering, in spite of rigour, succinct but weighed on. It was helpful to take a little series of pills in place of you. Set down precedence of mighty but unsure chemical reliance. Elements not scheduled. Arisen not meeting. A flame who plunged into defunct night help me to float down shaken but deserving no less than everything.

The hostile space around each name beckons. I would long to work on soundly besides. Who plunged into the night. At that time deserving no less than everything. Finally, I come to visit you with your slow gaze & deliberate blindsight. Your hair which was always fine is streaked with grey & adequate silence. No adapting, just a process unravelling itself soundly here in other people's minds. But they say nothing can grow beneath greatness anyway—the pastoral typifies—nothing can not get burnt. Anything shades up to difference or gradates nicely. I have not reached this stage for nothing. But not even now, completely wilful.[4] *When I say women don't need that kind of hurt for anything I mean it* not even as a way of joking.

Seeing you there has been some of the worst times of my life I wish I could get ~~knowledge of insanity~~ out of my head

Or else you think someone's pretending to be me which is so hurtful Your obstinacy is so hurtful when reality's obvious

[4] ~~I wish I could get you out of my head~~

Emily Critchley read for a PhD in contemporary American women's experimental poetry and philosophy at Cambridge University, where she won the John Kinsella–Tracy Ryan Prize for poetry in 2004. She has published poetry chapbooks with Arehouse Press, Bad Press, Dusie and Oystercatcher Press. Her latest collection, *Hopeful for Love are th' Impoverish'd of Faith*, is forthcoming from Torque Press, Southampton. Critchley regularly contributes poetry and feminist criticism to journals and anthologies, and in 2006 she organized the first festival for contemporary experimental women's poetry to be held in Cambridge. She teaches English literature, creative writing and theory at the University of Greenwich, London.

FRANCES KRUK

With coat hangers and live wires in hand, Frankenstein's secret girl bastards run through these poems spitting blood and oozing their calculated poisons. While each poem stems from different serial projects undertaken between 2004–2007, the sciatic pathway connecting them is rooted in the uneasy pathology addressed in my work as a whole. By uneasy pathology I refer to my recurring engagement with themes that cause tension or disquiet for myself or for others, from the exposition of viscera to the committing, witnessing, or experiencing of psychic, physical, or political violence that shapes alienated human existence. Confronting cultural malaises requires the recognition of poetry as a locus of resistance, of soothsaying. It is a revelator of raw forms and textures and realities that mean. There must be a material to realize this: in my case it is the body, in one form or another.

My position as a female body composing a text frequently seeps into what I write, despite anxieties about falling into the pits of what femininity is or is not purported to be, or whether or not female subjectivity is even relevant in a given poem. Grappling with this without losing sight of wider human problems, I am still a subject that cannot be erased or avoided, regardless of whoever feigns to speak in the poems. Any corporeal experience(s) of frustration and struggle, within or without myself, are always deeply engrained beneath my skin, and therefore cannot be entirely blocked out of my work. Gendered or not, this body is too honest to not spin the malice of poetry. Impish, body and poetry and language—with all their truths and lies and sugar-coatings—use each other as vessels of contempt against those who would use them to maintain oppressive false consciousness over all bodies—politically and/or artistically. Impish, because of the strangeness of confrontational tone and imagery pitched alongside potential secrets, giving the unshakeable feeling that a slow venom is operating: an enzymatic blockade to the opponent, a catalyst for the comrade. The material body and its contents are both the nervous source and the intended result of these poems—that is, refusal, mobilization, and re-making of what it lives in.

flux

fluxisourfabricdelayedcellular
gridsunfoldandsplayhibiscustan
glesaglassfulofsuspensiontenta
clesunfurledpetalsalltheethere
dbiosystemimpliedbysuchswirlan
redthisinfusionacollapseofplan
ttowatertobodyfromkettleaftert
henightprowlbetweenthecobblesa
ndsteelandtheneonandthecarswit
theirendlesseyesjustmovingmovi
movingmovingmovingmovingmovi
moving moving moving moving
moving moving moving moving
oving ng ing ing ing
in g ng n v
m g i g
v in g vig in
v i g vin g vng m
g i g n ng g m
m v v i v
o v h g l i
b v u v x s
b x c u v b v n
i o r o i
f u o i
aj u f l b ru c
flux is u fbric
grids un l r
flux is our fabric delayed ce
llular grids unfold and splay
hibiscus tangles a glassful o
f suspension tentacles unfurl
ed petals all the ethered bio
system implied by such swirls
ol red this infusion a collap
se of plant to water to body
from kettle after the night p
rowl between the cobbles and
steel and the neon and the ca
rs with their endless eyes ju
st moving moving moving movin

now is a time to storm. Shall I speak for thee
though rhetoric dismembers the very
reality it would portray.

gets worse.

tongue twigged
            n flickered to dirt to twitch
      to batter itself in śmiecie & błoto
                  so you must
            mouth
            sorry   my hole

            is bleeding i've lost it

i've nothing
to say

and meanwhile with no place in scummy
bandages to tuck a pen
      no words
      for golem just empty
crumples when he wakes:
there's nothing
to do
but wave your stumps
as if to perfume the room

            untouchable & unable
                  to touch   sure,
            Speak like hands

            when you're all bound & bleeding
            useless shuddering
cuts
in This tedious sampler means
            A body

stopp'd neither
use
nor ornament
blocked nothing
but blows
tho even blows come
through

closet

comfort of dozens of arms snaked through panty loops I wire my
content and with a glass I can listen and with a hole I can. for example,
if the shoe fits. a personal inventory of ways to address, redress, regress,
nudify documents. rattle knobs. seal flesh in dry clean plastic wrap. ring
rosies with appropriate fibres like those hand cut, hand sewn, a bloody
bias for scissors. hems released in seam undone. room to view under
where can I put this. of course. and dangle.

how to build your very own army

one death births
another terminal begins
with the tapping of her
wires gutted, short-circuited
        at most there's little left.

beauty is programmed
        language   not a specific feminine trait
chanelled into flesh
and bone the sear of man
        made junctions
            at each point of contact
                sharp metal spark of moving

electrons just tears flesh
evaporates blood
steams out
her
and the leftovers:
hollow
flask for filling
oh boys and their chemistry sets
the wunders of science
the power of technology
the pelvis a tabula rasa
point of insertion for new receptors
switch on
this motherboard made to command
the start of progress
by elimination
creation

slaver

the old crust funks my belly
its vinegar stink & novelettish scraps
say upheave while the rest rot
tired in bigbox stores & under 18
wheelers i'm a laugh
a minute with my outdated barbs
n wannabe dangertits flapping
all sheets in saleable winds
need changing need tearing

has alphahydroxy no use?
can't the worn bits be sizzled off
n all the stripped maw
clenched in those pages splat
new
for those of us still hungry

huddled in remainder bins over
flowing with cookbooks & yoga dvds
To break this body distract
    read and do words they say lie
shameful in unfashionable tomeyards
little zombie spines yapping silly
revolution silly say silly with mcstuffed mouth
or once more let leg drippings burn
what's unworthy i have
stomach for obliteration womb
for suffocation friendly face for fire
needs throwing

❖

Frances Kruk (b. 1981, Calgary) lives in London, where she works within various art forms and creates wee books for the occasional micro press yt communication. She has published *A Discourse on Vegetation & Motion* (Cambridge: Critical Documents, 2008), and is featured in *Shift & Switch: New Canadian Poetry* (Toronto: Mercury Press, 2005). Her poetry can be found in various literary journals—among them *fhole, onedit.net, West Coast Line, HOW2*—and she has contributed performative and site audio design work to the online journal of digital art and culture, horizonzero.ca. She has exhibited visual art and performed poetry and music internationally, and collaborated for several years in the multimedia collective Tar Disaster Project in Calgary, Canada.

MARIANNE MORRIS

It depresses me when someone says (and not without good reason), 'I don't *get* poetry,' as if it were locked in a box. Maybe I want a sledgehammer instead of a pen. I don't feel that poetic art is happening elsewhere, in another era—it is happening here, and now, and poems have the opportunity, thanks to there being enough of the right kind of people interested in them and writing them, to challenge the traditional boundaries of formal conveyance, to be perverse with content, tight with form, quick-witted, rhetorical—in short, to be really brilliant.

When I sit down to write a poem, I may have in mind any combination of the following:

> the day's news, the temperature of the air, the nature of things stirring my heart, something about caterpillars or spoons or missile shields, media obsessions like obesity or terrorism, an emotional image.

These things are tempered during the act of writing by:

> theoretical concerns e.g. Benjamin, "Truth is the death of intention", Rancière, "who to speak to or who not to speak to", negative capability, an idea of something being wrong or right, a line of just men, a humongous disappointment.

All this to say that the only reasonable way in which I am capable of explaining my poetry is -as movement-. This movement is the byproduct of the poet's constant search for extraordinary experience: in love, betrayal, adventure, pain, or speed (for example)—all believing it will yield him/her an increased capability with language—one that is closer, inevitably, to being more truly an expression of the poet's self, but closer also, crucially, to being nothing of him/her at all. Most poets will tell you that they are influenced by other poets, but what they are really influenced by is their own heart, by the hearts of others, and by drink (for example). Why are we the way we are? Why are particular moments beautiful? How am I going to transcribe this pressure?

I do not write what is called 'free verse'. In lieu of rhyme and meter, in my practice, it is the poem's visual composition that demarcates boundaries and prosodic constraints.

La Partida (The Game)

I take up begging—it's the way the music shifts, I stay up
going through jpegs. Lightning, orange of starting day, the
warmth of the heart, a sheet of muslin bells, something
lonely. It's the city that's done it to me. Purple and orange
and red. A lonely traveller. Then the lightning again. The
dawn. The overwhelming softness of something in water
colour, the wheat bells again. I sit in the silence, waiting
for the previous death to conclude.

                                          I flowered then by
stammering something, that was always the way. The drum
sounds a little, very gently and when its insistence grows
I have the feelings between my ribs, memories, more jpegs.

My body surges with electrical heat and goosebumps, rows
and rows of wheat where our beauty is permitted to roam
more or less freely, but not to be an observer, oh please
let it not be so. I cried out, I had done what I came to do
and the broken light fixture was a bird, up there against the
door frame, flying through a paper dimension. The closed
door and the cracks in the paint seem no obstruction. Seek
no more to make within hate, the weary may rest here now,
sentenced to much longing.

                                     Again and again it will be necessary
to butcher the lining of the vena cava, scrape out the venereal
muck, release more birds, forget about politics entirely, lend
definition to the atria, each tenderly in their turn, action is
remembered differently now. And to make more calls, well
that will be certified. The border abounds with social things,
their beckoning difficult now to understand.

The Russians Come

In the rockpool we viewed the instruments
that had just flashed on the screen, bouncing over cliffs
we monitored the screen until it came to life
the drill of death making destiny palpable I turned to you and laughed
your eyes were dead but there was the literary probability of love
khakis, chinos, sandy shirts. I had my top off. The Russians were
stirring up trouble, wanted
4,000 island inhabitants lined up ready for shooting by some
cut-off point, you said, there's no point
in hiding, as we shrugged off a narrow shrapnel death,
given that I died long ago.
I made a run for it, loosing grip from your sleeve
into the house
which trapped me variously. How disappeared our
Mediterranean thing, personally I blame your
shadows of staged invincibility.
So the Russians come, and with bazooka blow the door I
hide behind, but I decide, I won't be afraid, and I win.
The one with the bazooka gets it in the head with a guitar,
and I wake having survived, care for you dead.
        On the flipside the dream allowed me
to consider the ways in which certain modes of being were
infringements upon my sense of self. In between
rolling on waves of alcoholic sickness and
wanting to unravel the various mysteries of the gun it allowed me
to locate the points at which the various slats were canted.
I viewed the terrain without disappointment,
a kind of peaceful detachment, as of the dead when they rise
up to the firmament, watching gently the scenes unfold
below to their finishing lines.

from *Cocteau Turquoise Turning*

Turquoise

not knowing anything or her name. Rich
susurration of words at soil's thumby reach
and he gluey gibbers, love is here love has
still remained and nothing is mine alone.
Walks that brief mountain repeatedly, up
in four and down in seven repeatedly, God
ot's black mirage its culmination never to
culminate. Marriage shaped in the clouds
they appear white they bristle and pull off
themselves, in the sky live happy people,
thrashed in our image he bolsters thrashed
into this man's image, border crossing the
goo grabs at his shoes to threaten with murk
the entrust feverish body and sickness made
big with lacking swollen bones of starvation,
could have said the growth too late the growth
embittered in one soapy blast, hair included.
Awkward faces corral each other someone's
got to, blemish on the magic we try to tell
ourselves lies in glossy red finished box, as in
death so it goes in the life as well. Stuck to a
different sort of sticking place courage depends.

The she rinsed out of her she conjured, gated,
drew back the remains of the gathered curtain
hated in gold safeness, of infants, she dreamed
and grew upon wider and wider, to a gleaming
ball of orb-like beauty, the kind that generates
in self-reflection torrid and unuseful. Witty
wanderer a correctional medicine of tools and
chopped wood he might one day find for her
a partner, to kill by, the franked remains of her
first ghost, still alive and thriving in the rose

carriage of bones. Carries her in wisps of hits
of the mock cloth, to protect and to hiding bury
the enormous growing vat of loveliness to
scratch loneliness into its weaving heart, pink
and white and creaming to do for itself what
audiences do to lights the fleeting vital fled
comparisons that cut off from life. This state
unable to generate until the word fate to his
spirit placate used Cocteau. Blinded Cocteau
with the flash and generous spit of a needful
heart, torn in with scraps to be used in the end,
omissions, collisions, the greatness of plum sky

ignites. Collision me she pleads and beckons
unbeknownst to beckoning and ripped him
away from her heart, where underneath the
flesh removed in ripping ranged a vivid image
eyes like dark twins pooling into the fatness
of their sad seclusion. And that was Cocteau
widened with intensity staring up from wounds
self-inflict her rose upon the downs of trolling
quickened ease, the quest frenetic merciless,
their four eyes rolling in steaming studded
hiss of limbs seeking slake, do you know
me would you care to know me would I whether
care Turquoise considered without time enough
to know a self in lashings or stitches knowings
set out and unencumbered, to brown butter she
thought with eyes I am so controlled afraid I
gazed into the nervous camera shook me curls
up and curled down around a snake's teeth are
squarely mine, my father's form a lash of size
no mal to overcome, no man, unless the size
of moons and eyes of mine. The ones I know do
not venture into dialogue she to the mirror said.

Part Boutique

Christmas the warm cacophony of spend. Warm up to
the swing door, boost yourself through dripping wool,
busily fish out your list from the folds, you on a mission.
The list has items of white steel spearing the ice blue sky,
coloured multi-purpose LCD indicators, leather interiors,
onboard video recorder to film the faces of Scandinavians
as the airspace is leisurely penetrated, onboard
guns and so many bombs! Hypothetical orgasms.
In the boutique your gimlet overflows, air-con makes a
mess of your lungs. Annihilating the outside fit into a
spurt of more ice stars, the grammar belittles you on sale
a slew of rabidly gorgeous price tags elicit piracy
where tutu-adorned offspring twirl round mummy
in mini fur. Hold closer to me in the vague purport of
objects, to lessen the primp of aloneness we mock a
family. It is as you like it with your wireless credit terminal.
There are deep-fried balls of fat within glass canisters and
call-girls plummeting from the ceiling on aerial cords, there
are sparkling wings and diamond vodka and there are
combat aircraft and scented candles. Increasingly the
blood and turmoil signified is distanced from the price tag.
The boutique is now actually stationed in your office building!
All you need is turn right on exiting the canteen where
Victorian eggs and crystalline watch-faces careen beside
infallible turkey pork and cheese concoctions. The repeat
of certain chemicals will dance as nothing ever before has
danced in your intestinal tract, joyful assistants in leotards.
Mahmoud Ahmadinejad is doing the Oxford Street Christmas
lights. That is only funny because putting Persia on the map
will be the last thing you will do unless this language of power
becomes somehow eventually less sponsored, oh hands of
mine you are cold now wrapped round the icy jewelled egg.
Driving the
death of you in an SUV into something that looks
like pleasure. Behind you a cargo of meat and feathers and

fine-tailoring. Behind the sybaritic colour palette, a drastic
black that shines and dulls in equal measure, that giveth
e'en as it taketh away, inexplicably beset by neutralizing attributes.
It is the sum total of all desire, the coagulated shenanigan that
makes men into National Leaders, gears leisure time up,
glistening as people fellate the oblong metal tags. Oil
your guns, Chengdu!, shrieks the other, but both of them have
ceased to have names. This just in: all of the product
holdings companies have been consolidated, mooning you
by video-link, one fat state-forearm up the A-hole. What does
this mean in a wider context? That ideologies are clearer.
That selective economic resistance is jokes. That nothing
can stop the buyer.
Therefore as you were,
twirling in spit comprising the fishtail of your beluga ballgown,
umbrella raining fish jizz down your Swarovski cock accessory.

To buy or not to buy, that is not the question. The question
in a fit of language piques finally at democracy, having
just about had enough. A mess both in style and content.

❖

Marianne Morris was born in Toronto in 1981 and raised in London. She studied English Literature at Newnham College, Cambridge and is now undertaking research for a PhD at Dartington College of Arts/University College Falmouth. Together with Jow Lindsay and Jonathan Stevenson she founded Bad Press in 2002. Her published poetry includes: *Tutu Muse* (New York: Fly By Night Press, 2008); *A New Book From Barque Press, Which They Will Probably Not Print* (Cambridge: Barque Press, 2006); with Bad Press: *Cocteau Turquoise Turning* and *Fetish Poems* (2004); *Gathered Tongue* (2003); *Memento Mori* (2003); *Poems in Order* (2002).

SOPHIE ROBINSON

In poems I feel like I am almost always treading the line between the concept and my relation to it—as much as I am interested in investigating and exhausting a certain idea, object or mode of being. I am also interested in my subjective relationship to the world, and finding ways of expressing that relation in non-standard ways (poetically speaking). I don't believe that an experimental poetics must necessarily be devoid of emotion, sentiment, biography, self-expression, &c—and I'd say that most of the writers I admire the most bring these elements into their work as a part of their experimental practice (Frank O'Hara & Bernadette Mayer, to name my two most cherished).

I tend to work from those things—the personal, the everyday—and then begin a process of writing and rewriting which untangles those things from habitual language, or complicates them, in order to explore the politics around them and the implications of the given. This also, sometimes, brings me closer in proximity to the concept of 'feeling' than a more traditional/conventional 'confessional' or lyrical style might in that, by breaking with the language closest at hand to describe a given experience, 'irrational' connections are made which present the situation anew, and allow for a more dynamic response.

anecdotally yours

Countless, homeless, we look for new genders
in our dark dark our schizoid isolation
& ask please treat me with inappropriate
respect, embrace my poor nutrition my

nausea bones my belly which may or may
not be growing something [somatically
ruminating, rumbling, &c] or hit
the spacebar instead of – tidy, tidy

with sharp edges, badly in need of a
hero. Cutting holes in ourselves versus
buying large desktop organisers to

store our recollections of the past, of
all of the world slipping down the k-hole
of our minds, our tickly loose connections.

"Glisten, Glisten, glisten, glisten"
after John Keats & Adrienne Rich

Thump me restlessly against the darkling
Drum of your disquiet, pulse-rattle and
Wheeze a werewolf-hungry eye a
Stormy pounding chromosomal ache a
Scratch of needy charm neglected, named &
Filed away waiting, charring itself to ruin
To spoil in the zombie-fleckered dankness,
Wanting, chagrin grimace betraying urge,
Loosened hips to buck & smoothen,
Iron-down frottage, eiderdown merging,
Feathered to resurgent skin-scansion –
Read and comb the yearning emergency
To crest & crash, to splurge trembling the whole

World across the pane, to glitter patent &
Pattern itself as strings from gurning lips
To spell its listless etude toward the sky.

tetris heart

ear full of sounds we have plagiarised, your
face printed on a t-shirt above a
forgettable slogan, my tickly desire
transmitted via a homemade skirt. I

have been writing this poem for 6 hours.
The plastic bricks are not only durable,
they communicate our daily needs to
us. Comments, icons, avatars,—& your kitsch,

your eternal novelty, crackerprize charm,
I'd never cheat. We – play – like – this – down,
then left, flip horizontal. Hard captor,

my retro crush, freeze me DOWN & press START
pronto, save me from plunging elbow deep
into data, a love wrought in small units.

Winded by Love

And what hurt her damp hand touched with
Her nose in her arm –
her cut knees waste away below her
Those beyond tones, with sore-belted lips
Flower that last hip, drown hard in rebuke
Oily fingers in a jar, a legging-lover squatting
In the low-ribbed land, gingerly gurning towards
A peekaboo crotch vibrating against a useless

Void of understanding, the owl's head hung
At the sight of people going broken, let
My tape dispenser run long against my
Starred earlobe – you are a held place &
Your palms beg me not to gaze –
Swollen like dogs we will live forever
In this mess – malachite bellies held proud
And bare

Toward her, a cantata of grace (part one: suture)
For G.

If I were you and you were me I would
Turn and turn again, move my arms from left
To right, I would large I would small I would
Seek out all the danger. If I were me
And you were a tall blue thing a light coming
Out from the sides of all the sad then yes
I would stroke your ruffled feathers sleepy
And unknowing, blind in the bed which knows
Us, fucking or not – being us – your or
Me – is like getting away with it, laughing
then being slapped away like being told
we are too good – if I were you I would
disappear, would fright myself away – if
I were me I would beat myself across
Myself would find myself out and just say,
When you were a child you could not stay inside
And now you still must be caught and brought in
Clopping, cold and snotty from the wanting.
Play your games on a Wednesday scuff your dust
Do anything you would do if you were
you and I were me I would eat the whites
of your eggs your eyes and whisk the yolks out
to form themselves anew. Terror masses

around us – the whine of legitimate
lovemaking. I have accomplished only
you, am small and unable to shock. We
are here, chewing the courser fat to forget
the living freaks falling down like zips like
propositions – FRANCE I LOVE YOU in food,
sour and sighed, and if I were you I would
move to a society dead of western
grace – and yes we shall move with our
motivations for moving writ large across
the screen as in a silent movie. I
Scratch myself deep inside the thicket of
your charm and anything alright still
Remains tough scuffing your oxfords
Beyond frigidity the meaning of which
Is caught in my wing and we acre carrying
The sky as emptiness, sustained beneath,
Sour and communicative…nobody's
Intimate taste is perverse, and a lusty
Burning has set in between my scars, a
Crippling freedom braided into us, skirting
Savagely the legitimating reports
Of our deaths. If I were me I would
Be a bloated male goddess, as emotional
As I am British. If I were you I would go soft
Under the night's shadow, I would kill the
Prose, I would kill the film, I would sick up
All the silence. If you were me I would
Smell you automatically for
What you are, manhandled automatically
in the summer of individual problems, unable
To talk anything out in a meaningful
Or sustained way we die faster than all
The other discourses. I have been growing
This hair since I was eleven and I
Quite like it, as animals like their
Cellars. If I were you I would make

Myself my pastime, young and difficult
As I am. Constellations of honour
Arrange themselves above us as we eat
At the heels of poetry & I splay
myself dizzy with the effort of
Living like a sexy patriot spasming
down my spine. This light has never been in
my control, my living pose unearthed
and taking form in slow in fast inside
the pulse of your neck in repose,
rigid with freedom. If I were you
I'm not sure I'd stay, but that does not
Make your lascivious goodbye any more
Charming.

Suicide Tuesday

A regime devoted to time
embodied in the colour of a wall or running
repeatedly into yourself
spattering thighs; knee-deep in lard
breath-by-breath attack
starving for a digital release I
am accurate – moot musculature –
diligently flowing
outward away from posterity whipped
into relief the texture of
beaten leather;
suction cups, monster artists stuck to myriad
bathroom floors as a naïve
defence against anxiety –
Billie Holliday vox
tremors soaked in deep red quiet amid
the itchy knife
of emotional compromise –
inventories of abstracted
feeling burned into grids as markers of
claustrophobic unlovability, which
worn as a crown demands
the question
why am I here –
what did my tidy heart want
to witness?

❖

Sophie Robinson was born in 1985. She has an MA in Poetic Practice from Royal Holloway, University of London. Her work has appeared in *The Reality Street Book of Sonnets* (Hastings: Reality Street Editions, 2008) and *Voice Recognition: 21 Poets for the 21st Century* (Tarset: Bloodaxe Books, 2009). Her first book, *a*, came out from Les Figues, Los Angeles, in 2009. Robinson lives and works in London, where she is currently completing a PhD.

ACKNOWLEDGEMENTS

The poems in this anthology are previously unpublished, and are copyright ©
2010 by the authors, except where noted below.

Sascha Akhtar: 'I–Body 4' and 'I–Body 5' were first published in *How2*.

Isobel Armstrong: 'After Iraq: reflections on a train', 'Second Desert Collages',
'Third Desert Collages' and 'Fourth Desert Collages' were all previously
published in *Desert Collages* (Cambridge: Equipage, 2007); 'Defining Deaths'
previously appeared in *Shearsman*. Copyright © Isobel Armstrong, 2007.

Caroline Bergvall: 'Cropper' first appeared in the online Norwegian magazine
Nypoesi (#3, 2006). It was accompanied by a piece called 'Scroll', a series of
ink drawings created with Marit Münzberg as a Flash piece. A revised version,
also in collaboration with Münzberg as designer, was published as a chapbook
in a limited edition by Torque Press (Southampton, 2008). Text as printed here
copyright © Caroline Bergvall, 2006.

Elisabeth Bletsoe: 'The Birds of the Sherborne Missal' was previously published
in *Landscape from a Dream* (Exeter: Shearsman Books, 2008). Copyright ©
Elisabeth Bletsoe, 2008.

Andrea Brady: 'Still Hanging on Clinton's Second Visit' and 'End of Days' were
first published in *Notre Dame Review* 28 (Summer/Fall 2009): 4–6.

Emily Critchley: 'When I say I believe women' has appeared in *How2, Pilot,
Openned Anthology*, and *Archive of the Now*. It also appeared in a chapbook of the
same name, published by Bad Press, Cambridge, in 2006. Copyright © Emily
Critchley, 2006.

Claire Crowther: 'Once Troublesome' and 'A Seafront Wake for the Postwar'
first appeared in the *London Review of Books*; 'Young Woman With Scythe' and
'Books (A Friend I Had)' first appeared in *Shearsman*.

Carrie Etter: 'Prairie' and 'A Starkness in Late Afternoon' first appeared in
Shearsman; 'Paternal' first appeared in *Bombay Gin*; 'Divining for Starters (71)'
first appeared in *Gists & Piths*.

Catherine Hales: 'across the', 'than venice', 'divination', 'divergences' and
'context' were previously published in *hazard or fall* (Exeter: Shearsman Books,
2010). Copyright © Catherine Hales, 2010.

Frances Kruk: 'flux' and 'now is a time...' first appeared in *onedit* 8; 'slaver'
first appeared in *Pilot*; 'how to build...' first appeared in *West Coast Line* 44;
'closet' first appeared in *clobber* (London: yt communication, 2006; copyright
© Frances Kruk, 2006). An earlier version of this last poem was also published
in *onedit* 5.

Rachel Lehrman: Selections of 'Nightscape' appeared in *The Drunken Boat,* 6.3–4 (Fall/Winter 2006). http://www.thedrunkenboat.com/rlehrman.html

Sophie Mayer: 'Import/Export' and 'Zero/navel' were previously published in the collection *Her Various Scalpels* (Exeter: Shearsman Books, 2009). Copyright © Sophie Mayer, 2009.

Marianne Morris: 'La Partida' and 'The Russians Come' previously appeared in *Tutu Muse* (New York: Fly By Night Press, 2007); 'Turquoise' previously appeared in *Cocteau Turquoise Turning* (Cambridge: Bad Press, 2004). Copyright © Marianne Morris, 2002, 2007.

Wendy Mulford: 'I China Am' was composed for performance (voice and music-drone) at the Arnolfini Gallery, Bristol, December 2006, for the inauguration of the Black Mountain College anniversary exhibition. It previously appeared in the collection *The Land Between* (Hastings: Reality Street Editions, 2009). Copyright © Wendy Mulford, 2009. Thanks to Reality Street Editions for permission to reprint.

Frances Presley: 'Learning Letters' previously appeared in the collection *Lines of sight* (Exeter: Shearsman Books, 2009). Copyright © Frances Presley, 2009.

Anne Reckin: 'As If That Way' and 'Fabric' first appeared in *Shearsman*.

Denise Riley: both poems printed here were previously published in *Selected Poems* (London: Reality Street Editions, 2000). Copyright © Denise Riley, 2000. Thanks to Reality Street Editions for permission to reprint them here.

Zoë Skoulding: The title 'The Museum for Disappearing Sounds' is drawn from R. Murray Schafer, *The soundscape: our sonic environment and the tuning of the world* (Destiny Books [1977], 1994); an early draft of this poem appeared in *Agenda*. 'The Old Walls', 'The Baths of Amnesia' and 'Castle' were previously published in *Remains of a Future City* (Bridgend: Seren Books, 2008). Thanks to Seren Books for permission to reprint them here. Copyright © Zoë Skoulding, 2008.

Carol Watts: 'Hare' was first published in *Dusie*: Issue Six, 2:2 (2007). http://www.dusie.org/watts.html Thanks to Susana Gardner, editor of *Dusie*.